MW00810030

LUTHER'S CHRISTOLOGICAL LEGACY

CHRISTOCENTRISM AND THE CHALCEDONIAN TRADITION

THE PÈRE MARQUETTE
LECTURE IN THEOLOGY
2017

LUTHER'S CHRISTOLOGICAL LEGACY

CHRISTOCENTRISM AND THE CHALCEDONIAN TRADITION

Johannes Zachhuber

MARQUETTE
UNIVERSITY
PRESS

LIBRARY OF CONGRESS CATALOGING-IN-PUBLICATION DATA

NAMES: Zachhuber, Johannes, author.
TITLE: Luther's Christological legacy : Christocentrism and the Chalcedonian tradition / by Johannes Zachhuber.
DESCRIPTION: first [edition]. | Milwaukee, Wisconsin : Marquette University Press, 2017. |
SERIES: The Père Marquette lecture in theology ; 2017 | Includes bibliographical references.
IDENTIFIERS: LCCN 2017049560 | ISBN 9781626005068 (hardcover : alk. paper)
SUBJECTS: LCSH: Luther, Martin, 1483-1546. | Jesus Christ—Person and offices. | Jesus Christ—History of doctrines.
CLASSIFICATION: LCC BR333.5.C4 Z33 2017 | DDC 232.092—dc23
LC RECORD AVAILABLE AT: https://urldefense.proofpoint.com/v2/url?u=https-3A__lccn.loc.gov_2017049560&d=DwIFg&c=S1d2Gs1Y1NQV8Lx35_Qi5FnTH2uY-Wyh_OhOS94IqYCo&r=hokKgJ4JxWGN8r507i6qR6wpZ-D_MmlVVO57591llHQ&m=Fu3Y4nQ-aWLxqbF8h65lDOdMKWGCOZqNuYtv4wHaREw&s=drxyaHXeNqS9tIkPuVPUtf_8i8fX6ICqryFQ8VQ8fuk&=

© 2017 Marquette University Press
Milwaukee WI 53201-3141
All rights reserved.
founded 1916

♾The paper used in this publication meets the minimum requirements of the American National Standard for Information Sciences—Permanence of Paper for Printed Library Materials, ANSI Z39.48-1992.

Association of American University Presses

FOREWORD

The 2017 Père Marquette Lecture in Theology is the forty-eighth in a series commemorating the missions and explorations of Père Jacques Marquette, SJ (1637-75). This series of lectures was begun in 1969 under the auspices of the Marquette University Department of Theology. The Joseph A. Auchter Family Endowment Fund had endowed the lecture series. Joseph Auchter (1894-1986), a native of Milwaukee, was a banking and paper industry executive and a long-time supporter of education. The fund was established by his children as a memorial to him.

JOHANNES ZACHHUBER

Johannes Zachhuber is Professor of Historical and Systematic Theology, University of Oxford, Faculty of Theology and Religion. He specializes in two main areas of research: the Eastern Patristic tradition up to John of Damascus and modern theology from the Reformation to the present, with a special interest in nineteenth-century German theology. The present lecture provides an example of his efforts to unite historical research on Patristic writings and currents of modern thought, in this case the Christology of Martin Luther. But he has pursued similar research in other areas: theological anthropology, ecclesiology, and the relation of theological to philosophical developments. His current research projects have to do, first, with the emergence of a Christian philosophy in doctrinal debates following the Council of Chalcedon, and second, with systematic-theological reflection on the significance of individuality for the Christian faith.

Among his writings are *Theology as Science in Nineteenth-Century Germany: From F.C. Baur to Ernst Troeltsch* (Oxford: Oxford University Press, 2013) and *Human Nature in Gregory of Nyssa: Philosophical Background and Theological Significance* (Leiden: Brill, 1999; paperback, 2014). He is one of the editors of *The Oxford Research Encyclopedia on Martin Luther*, 3 vols. (Oxford: Oxford University Press, 2017).

Robert M. Doran, S.J.

LUTHER'S CHRISTOLOGICAL LEGACY

CHRISTOCENTRISM AND THE CHALCEDONIAN TRADITION

Johannes Zachhuber

CONTENTS

1 Introduction

It is not easy to miss the irony of a Père Marquette Lecture given in commemoration of the five-hundredth anniversary of the Reformation. I have been unable to find any specific comments made by Jacques Marquette about the Reformation, about Martin Luther or about Protestantism, but it is safe to assume that he would not have held favorable views about any of those. After all, his order, the Society of Jesus, had been founded with the express aim to counter the advances made by the Protestants in central Europe and beyond, and he was surely aware of all the theological reasons underlying this agenda. I suspect Father Marquette would also have found it difficult to imagine that one day, centuries after his death, a University and indeed a lecture series would be named after him, but assuming for the sake of the argument that he was able to imagine such future renown attached to his person, what would he have made of the fact that one such lecture would be given in honor of the beginnings of the Reformation movement five hundred years after it took place?

It could possibly be quite fascinating to start speculating here, but I shall resist the temptation and instead confine myself to the observation that, whatever precise thoughts Father Marquette might have entertained, they would surely serve to highlight that memorial events such as ours are never innocent or taking place without a context. For centuries, remembering the Reformation was, at the very least, a starkly partisan exercise.[1] For those who saw themselves as scions of that movement, such commemoration was happy, festive, and even triumphalist, while for those looking back to those same sixteenth-century developments with sadness, even trauma given the breakup of ecclesiastical unity in the West, the memory was inevitably painful and unwelcome.

Commemorations of Luther and the Reformation were divisive in other ways too. Especially throughout the nineteenth century, they were often taken into the service of national narratives supposedly proving the superiority of Protestant nations over the Catholic competitors.[2] This strategy later backfired rather spectacularly as, following Germany's troubled history in the early twentieth century, Luther would now appear at the origins of many of those fateful political and social tendencies holding back his country's development by his endorsement of pre-modern, patriarchal authoritarian structures, his "peasant's mistrust of money," as Max Weber put it,[3] while stirring his countrymen's most notorious

---

1   Tal Howard, *Remembering the Reformation: An Inquiry into the Meanings of Protestantism* (Oxford: Oxford University Press, 2016).

2   Howard, *Remembering the Reformation*, 66–92.

3   Max Weber, *The Protestant Ethic and the Spirit of Capitalism*, trans. Talcott Parsons (London: Routledge, 2001), 166, n. 11.

emotions through his violent anti-Judaism.[4] Marxist historians focused on his alliance with the princes in the peasants' war, and so forth.

1 Why Commemorate the Reformation Today?

Given this controversial patrimony, I am conscious that it does not go without saying that a Catholic University would invite a Protestant, Lutheran theologian to speak in commemoration of the origins of the Reformation. It reflects the enormous progress that has been made in ecumenical conversations and ecumenical rapprochement over the past fifty years. This progress is perhaps most impressively reflected in the Joint Declaration on the Doctrine of Justification, signed in 1999, stating that in the very question that lay at the center of past division and separation in the sixteenth century, no basis for mutual condemnation remained.

We often take this for granted today, and some have more recently started dismissing this progress as endangering the purity of their own traditions. Looking at the half millennium that has passed since Luther started what was to become the Reformation with its often open hostility between Protestants and Catholics, it seems evident to me that no one should belittle what has been achieved by the ecumenical

---

4   Thomas Kaufmann, *Luthers Juden* (Stuttgart: Reclam, 2014).

movement. Yet our very ability to perceive the bonds uniting us as Christians as stronger than the issues that may still divide us also raises the question of what significance a commemoration of the Reformation can still possess. What is the value, what is the need for such commemoration? Is it merely, in George Santayana's famous phrase, because those who cannot remember the past are condemned to repeat it? Or is there something genuinely worthwhile remembering about the Reformation? And if so, how can we identify it without falling back into an antagonism of Christian confessions?

When the ecumenical movement began, a century ago – even when the Catholic Church officially opened itself up to it, about fifty years ago – most of those engaged in those conversations were firmly rooted in their own traditions. Many European territories at that time still persevered more or less in the same confessional structures that had been established in the seventeenth century. Western ecumenism thus resembled a peace conference after an overly long and painful war. There was longing for partnership and friendship instead of opposition and hostility; there was also, it is true, hope for the restoration of full ecclesiastical communion, but the overall religious situation was in reality fairly static, dominated by long-established religious identities which in many cases overlapped with cultural and national identities.

In the meantime, the situation has changed dramatically. Those relatively static confessional structures have been all but shattered, and what remains of them is increasingly looking certain to disappear within a generation. For few people today, especially among the younger generation, religious identity is provided by their culture or even their family background. For an increasing number, by contrast, religious identity has become a question of personal search, experience, and ultimately decision. Much has been written about this development, and I have no need and no interest to discuss its wider implications in the present place. It seems to me, however, that its consequences for the future of ecumenical dialogue have not been sufficiently reflected on. Yet they seem rather obvious. For ecumenical enthusiasts of the previous generation, the benefits from studying and appreciating each other's theological insights seemed evident: it was a form of enriching their own Protestant or Catholic identities. It probably never occurred to most of them that somebody might ask why, if they liked the ideas and the forms of worship of the other tradition so much, they would not themselves prefer to become Protestant or Catholic.

Today, by contrast, in many Western countries this latter question is never far away for anyone dealing with ecumenical issues. This, it would seem, is simply the result of the collapse of confessional cultures and the emerging need for individuals to decide for themselves on their religious orientation. Ecumenical dialogue enters into crisis mode in this situation as those who would have to participate in them increasingly fall into two groups: those who treat the subtleties of theological difference as unimportant (or may not even know about them any longer) and those who feel that, given the decision they have made, these differences are the very foundation of their religious identities. The newly converted Catholic will, understandably, think of her faith as decidedly "non-Protestant," and the same goes for many others following their personal faith journey. Any mitigation of the purity of this confession in the interest of ecumenical understanding, in this perspective, runs directly counter to the person's deeply-held faith.

We should not be surprised, then, that this development has raised fundamental questions about the ecumenical process that dominated the twentieth century. Yet however serious these problems may be and wherever their solution may lie, it is arguable that the changes to the Western religious fabric in our own time open up, in one sense, the potential for a rediscovery of the Reformation period itself insofar as the latter, too, was a period in which religious identity often relied on individual decision more than inculturation. Thus far, the sixteenth century was different, by and large, from the religious equilibrium that established itself in Central Europe after the Peace of Westphalia in 1648 with its infamous principle of *cuius regio eius et religio* ("whose realm, his religion") and which continued to exist in European societies well into the post-war period.

It seems to me, therefore, that one of the more hopeful ways forward for ecumenical dialogue today is to re-establish the century of the Reformation as a time of theological, religious, and existential decisions that had to be taken and which could be taken one way or another. To conceptualize the Reformation in this way carries the hope of recovering its theological ethos; the questions of the participants in those debates can become our questions too even though we will have to recognize, inevitably, that we ask them in our own time and thus in different ways and with different options. In this way, remembering the controversies of the sixteenth century can help us better understand the decisions we ourselves have to take, one way or another, in our own time.

Such a reconstruction of the Reformation as a time of theological decision has the advantage of being able to recover the issues underlying those controversies in their theological significance while retaining respect for each side. It is not a position of theological relativism as it recognizes the need to make theological judgments at the individual as well as the communal level, but it reckons with the fact that different decisions could be made in good faith back then as well as now.

Such a form of ecumenism can perhaps take its cue from the great Greek theologian Origen. His opponent, a second-century philosopher called Celsus, had adduced the large number of Christian sects or schools (αἱρέσεις) as proof against the truth of the new religion. Origen, however, would have nothing of it. It is true, he concedes, that there are many schools within Christianity, but there are also many schools within medicine and philosophy and, actually, also in Judaism. The reason is, he speculates, that "schools of different kinds have never originated from any matter in which the principle involved was not important and beneficial to human life." These different schools in Christianity, then, arose, according to the Alexandrine thinker,

> … not at all as the result of faction and strife, but through the earnest desire of many literary men to become acquainted with the doctrines of Christianity. The consequence of which was, that, taking in different acceptations those discourses which were believed by all to be divine, there arose schools, which received their names from those individuals who admired, indeed, the origin of Christianity, but who were led, in some way or other, by certain plausible reasons, to discordant views.[5]

While Origen may well underplay the confrontational dimension of theological controversy about the right understanding of the faith, his affirmation that "discordant views" can be taken for "plausible reasons" and by the "earnest desire" of many indi-

---

5   Origen, *Contra Celsum*, II, 12.

vidual people is salutary and has too often been neglected in the history of the Christian Church.

These reflections lead me directly to my topic for
this lecture. Before entering into details, however,
let me pause briefly for one further clarification. In
choosing to address the continuing importance of
the Reformation along these lines, I consciously opt
for a theological approach to this historical movement. I do not think such an approach is the only
legitimate one. Scholars and intellectuals trying to
ascertain the importance of these sixteenth-century
developments have looked at various factors including political, social, economic, and broadly cultural
ones. They all have their right and can help shed
light on our understanding of a crucial period in
European history. Part of my reason for focusing
on theology is, inevitably, that I am a theologian by
training and thus speak of what I know and understand best.

Yet there is a broader point as well. I am firmly
convinced that the Reformation, whatever political,
social or economic issues played into its unfolding
– or were magnified by it – was at heart a religious
movement, and therefore needs to be analyzed and
understood along those lines if it is to be understood
at all.[6] A theological approach to the movement that
took its beginning five hundred years ago in a small
place in central Germany, is not just any angle that

---

6   Euan Cameron, *The European Reformation*, 2nd ed.
     (Oxford: Oxford University Press, 2012), 437.

can be chosen; it is arguably central for our understanding of what happened then and how it can still
be important for us today.

2 The Centrality of Christ in Luther's Theology

The theological answer I am going to propose is this,
that at the bottom of Luther's theological position
lay a strong and uncompromising affirmation of the
absolute centrality of the person of Jesus Christ for
the Christian faith. In this sense, the principle, slo-
gan or motto "Christ alone" (*solus Christus*) is the
culmination of the other three, similar phrases –
Scripture alone (*sola scriptura*); by faith alone (*sola
fide*); by grace alone (*sola gratia*) – which are often
associated with Reformation theology. The centrality of Luther's fixation on the person of Jesus Christ
as the one, single redeemer of humankind will, I
hope, open a perspective for the commemoration of
Luther and his Reformation that should be of interest and concern for Protestants and Catholics alike.

This centrality of Jesus Christ for Luther's thought
is immediately and impressively evident from his so-
called Smalcald Articles. This is a text the reformer
drafted in 1537; it was intended as a confession of
faith for a general council which at the time Pope
Paul III sought to convene.[7] As is well known, the

---

7   Werner Führer, *Die Schmalkaldischen Artikel* (Tübin-
    gen: Mohr Siebeck, 2009), 7–13.

Council only took place from 1545, in Trent, and then without Protestant participation. Yet in the previous decade, there was still some hope that such a gathering could heal the growing rift in Western Christianity, though Luther himself was sceptical.[8] Be this, however, as it may, the significance of the text is its apparent intent to summarize key principles of the Christian faith from Luther's own perspective. It was later integrated into the Book of Concord, the major collection of Lutheran confessional texts and has therefore retained a special importance for members of that church.

Right at the beginning of this document, after the enumeration of some consensual dogmatic foundations to which I shall return, Luther emphasizes the primacy of the person of Jesus Christ in words that permit no ambiguity:

The first and chief article

1] *That Jesus Christ, our God and Lord, died for our sins, and was raised again for our justification*, Rom. 4:25.

2] And *He alone is the Lamb of God which taketh away the sins of the world*, John 1:29; and *God has laid upon Him the iniquities of us all*, Is. 53:6.

---

8   Ibid. Christopher Spehr, *Luther und das Konzil: Zur Entwicklung eines zentralen Themas in der Reformationszeit* (Tübingen: Mohr Siebeck, 2010), 454–505.

3] Likewise: *All have sinned and are justified without merit [freely, and without their own works or merits] by His grace, through the redemption that is in Christ Jesus, in His blood*, Rom. 3:23f.

4] Now, since it is necessary to believe this, and it cannot be otherwise acquired or apprehended by any work, law, or merit, it is clear and certain that this faith alone justifies us as St. Paul says, Rom. 3:28: *For we conclude that a man is justified by faith, without the deeds of the Law.* Likewise 3:26: *That He might be just, and the Justifier of him which believeth in Christ.*

5] Of this article nothing can be yielded or surrendered [nor can anything be granted or permitted contrary to the same], even though heaven and earth, and whatever will not abide, should sink to ruin. *For there is none other name under heaven, given among men whereby we must be saved*, says Peter, Acts 4:12. *And with His stripes we are healed*, Is. 53:5. And upon this article all things depend which we teach and practice in opposition to the Pope, the devil, and the [whole] world. Therefore, we must be sure concerning this doctrine, and not doubt; for otherwise all is lost, and the Pope and devil and all things gain the victory and suit over us.[9]

---

9   Martin Luther, *The Smalcald Articles. Book of Concord* [http://bookofconcord.org/smalcald.php].

One does not need to apply much subtle interpretation to sense the weight of significance, even urgency, that is here attached to the confession of the singular importance and centrality of Jesus Christ for the Christian faith. This insistence has its roots, as is also immediately evident, in the connection, even identification, that Luther established between the person of the savior and his work, the salvation of humanity. Jesus is uniquely central to the Christian faith because Christianity promises redemption, and he is the one and only person who offers this gift. In this way, we can also perceive how Luther's emphasis on Christ alone led him to the postulation of the need to rely on faith over against any attempt to earn salvation by means of good works.

This last observation may perhaps begin to answer a question that is otherwise as mysterious as it is troubling. The question is this. Why should the insistence that Jesus Christ stands in an unrivaled position at the center of the Christian faith be controversial? After all, the centrality of faith in Jesus Christ is perhaps the one assumption that has been shared by Christians at all times and in all places since the time of the New Testament. Yet for Luther, accepting this principle had a ring of exclusivity that it did not always have. "Christ alone" was therefore incompatible with many practices accepted by the Church in his own time, notably the selling of indulgences, but also a particular way of venerating the saints, of celebrating mass, and ultimately of under-

standing the Church and, specifically, the institution
of the papacy. That is why he could write that "upon
this article all things depend which we teach and
practice in opposition to the Pope, the devil, and the
whole world."

But is this not merely a misunderstanding or, at
best, hyperbole? Was Luther unable properly to
perceive the religious and theological justification of
these practices? Was his protest the result of ecclesial
malpractices and abuses, thus understandable but
mistaken in its sweeping generalization? Was he perhaps simply in error or, worse, guided by intuitions
that are opposed to those held continuously by the
Church? Or, finally, did he contribute radically new
insights opening up a new chapter in the history of
the Church and of the Christian faith? All these
answers have been proposed, but none of them has
found universal acceptance, and thus the theological
problem raised by Luther's insistence that a proper
articulation of the centrality of Jesus Christ for the
Church leads to a radical critique of the entirety of
Christian existence, both personal and in community, remains as open to this day as it remains urgent.

In this lecture, I cannot address let alone solve
these fundamental questions. Instead I shall explore
Luther's theological commitment to *solus Christus* by
investigating his understanding of Christology, the
doctrine of the person of Jesus Christ. This doctrine
took its shape in the early Church; fundamental for
most later theologians are the decisions of the Coun-

cil of Chalcedon (451), which decreed that Jesus was fully divine and fully human in one, individual person.

Luther accepted this position and, as we shall see, made it clear time after time that for him it was the basis on which alone the unique significance of the person of the savior could be understood. What is perhaps more, he went out of his way to emphasize, time after time, that on this issue there was no difference of opinion between him and his theological opponents. In the *Smalcald Articles*, he laconically stated that "not the Father, nor the Holy Ghost but the Son became man."[10] In more detail, he wrote in his *Confession Concerning Christ's Supper* (1528):

> I believe and know that Scripture teaches us that the second person in the Godhead, viz. the Son, alone became true man ...

> Also that God the Son assumed not a body without a soul, as certain heretics have taught, but also the soul, i.e. full, complete humanity, and was born the promised true seed or child of Abraham and of David and the son of Mary by nature, in every way and form a true man, as I am myself and every other man, except that he came without sin, by the Holy Spirit of the Virgin Mary alone.

> And that this man became true God, as one eternal, indivisible person, of God and man, so that

---

10   Luther, *The Smalcald Articles*.

> Mary the holy Virgin is a real, true mother not
> only of the man Christ, as the Nestorians teach,
> but also of the Son of God ...[11]

Texts of this sort abound throughout Luther's
works; they indicate his commitment to Chalcedonian Christology. He certainly had no intention to
abolish or radically alter the terms of reference with
regard to these foundations of the church's faith.
Any study of Luther's Christology must start from
this recognition.

A first question, therefore, is how this traditional
doctrine underwrites Luther's specific understanding of the role of Jesus Christ in the life of the believer. Intriguingly, Luther gives many hints that a
proper understanding of the doctrine of Jesus Christ
is the foundation of theology as such, but he does
not, for the most part, engage in the technicalities
of Christology. This means that his more specifically
Christological ideas have to be pieced together from
a variety of writings that overtly deal with other topics. While this can appear tedious, however, it has
the advantage that those texts display directly the

---

11   LW 37, 361–62. Cf. LW 34, 207–209. Martin
     Luther, *Luther's Works*, edited by Jaroslav Pelikan et al.
     (St. Louis: Concordia, 1955–2015), is cited con-
     ventionally as LW. Martin Luther, *D. Martin Luthers
     Werke: kritische Gesamtausgabe* (Weimar: Böhlau,
     1883–2009); the Weimar edition of Luther's works is
     conventionally known as the *Weimarer Ausgabe* (Wei-
     mar edition) and cited as WA.

close connection between Luther's Christological ideas and the grand themes of his theology. This task of composing a picture of Luther's Christology from a wide range of his polemical, exegetical, even his poetic texts is taken up in the following chapter.

The results from this analysis will then provide the basis for a more systematic enquiry into the structure of Luther's Christology in chapter three. This section will also take into account those texts in which Luther dealt more technically with Christological doctrine. It seeks to address a second question that poses itself to the student of Luther's Christology. Given the reformer's twin claims that his Christology is entirely traditional *and* underwriting his Christocentric theology as a whole, how is it possible that the ensuing conception of Christian faith and practice in many ways differs from what has been accepted by the Catholic Church for a long time? Can a closer investigation of his Christology shed some light on this difficulty? The answer that will emerge is initially somewhat ambivalent. Closer inspection will reveal that, while Luther's affirmation of the Chalcedonian tradition is recurrent and sincere, he is willing to push against its limits in the interest of securing the *solus Christus* as he understood it.

Two further chapters will seek to clarify these findings. Chapter four will put Luther's Christology into conversation with Patristic debates which witness similar tensions ultimately leading to mutual condemnations and exclusion. The final chapter will ask in a more systematic key how far Christological doctrine can underwrite the unique significance the Church gives to the person of Jesus Christ and what this means for our appreciation of Luther's Christology today.

2 Luther's Christology across His Writings

Luther notoriously did not author a theology in systematic form although his thought is by no means lacking in internal coherence.[12] In this he resembles more the Church Fathers of the first millennium than the scholastic theologians of the Middle Ages who had shaped the intellectual world the reformer inherited. Like Athanasius and Augustine, Luther developed his theological vision through his highly polemical engagement in a series of controversies, which often makes it hard to separate deeply held theological convictions from the rhetorical acumination of a heated debate. At the same time, the biblical and exegetical cast of the reformer's thought – guiding him where the scriptural text leads – creates difficulties of interpretation that are all too familiar to the scholar of the Biblicist authors of the Patristic age, such as Origen or John Chrysostom.

Any attempt to reconstruct Luther's Christology faces these well-known problems; in fact, it faces them to a higher degree. There is a wealth of references to Christology and to Christological themes throughout Luther's sprawling oeuvre – the most

---

12   For a comprehensive treatment of Luther's theology, cf. Bernhard Lohse, *Martin Luther's Theology: Its Historical and Systematic Development*, trans. Roy A. Harrisville (Minneapolis, MN: Augsburg Fortress, 1999).

complete edition of his works, the so-called *Weimar-er Ausgabe*, comprises over one hundred volumes. As we shall see, a good case can be made that Christology is something like the lynchpin holding important strands of his theology together. Nevertheless, there is no single, classical or sustained treatment of Christology that would serve as the obvious starting point for any such reconstruction. There are, admittedly, some academic disputations from the late 1530s and early 1540s purporting to develop Luther's Christological thought in a more scholastic and thus inevitably more systematic form. Yet while they are important documents to be taken into account when seeking to understand Luther's Christological teaching, they are too late and too marginal to serve as a systematic point of departure. They cannot and should not replace the wealth of Christological thought that can be assembled from across the breadth of Luther's writings documenting his evolving thought since his early days as a professor of theology at Wittenberg University. Some scholars have consequently argued for the need to give a diachronic account of Luther's Christology. Notably, such an approach has been taken in Marc Lienhard's most comprehensive and still unsurpassed treatment of the topic.[13] In what follows, I shall nevertheless at-

---

13   Marc Lienhard, *Martin Luthers Christologisches Zeugnis: Entwicklung und Grundzüge seiner Christologie*, trans. Robert Wolff (Göttingen: Vandenhoeck & Ruprecht, 1979).

tempt a somewhat more systematic picture without, I hope, neglecting the development, the nuances, and indeed the tensions in Luther's writings.

In doing so, I shall inscribe Luther's approach to Christology into a threefold arc encompassing the believer's encounter with the suffering Jesus (1), the encounter of God in Jesus (2), and the encounter with the victorious Christ (3). All three must be seen as forming a tensional unity, not detached from each other but not forced into a systematic straightjacket either. They are bracketed, not least, by Luther's firm focus on salvation through Christ as the basis giving his entire theology a clear sense of direction.

1 Jesus Christ and Human Suffering

From Luther's earliest theological reflections, the centrality for his thought of the suffering of Jesus is evident.[14] This theological insistence has to be understood against a long history in Western theology of hesitation to acknowledge the full reality of Christ's suffering in the passion going right back to the Arian controversy of the fourth century.[15] That anti-Arian writers should caution against the idea that Christ suffered on the cross is perhaps unsur-

---

14   Ibid. 37–44, 88–97.

15   Paul Gondreau, *The Passions of Christ's Soul in the Theology of St Thomas Aquinas* (Münster: Aschendorff, 2002), 47–66.

prising: after all, the weakness of Christ's incarnate humanity was routinely cited by those opposed to the faith of Nicaea in support of their degradation of Christ's divinity. Few anti-Arian authors admittedly went as far as Hilary of Poitiers, who argued that in his Incarnation Christ did not at all experience pain. Yet for medieval authors, who often did not know many Greek Patristic texts but considered Hilary a major authority, his views were of great importance.

In Book X of his treatise *On the Trinity*, Hilary addressed the issue of Christ's suffering in the passion as a possible argument against his full divinity. His solution: the suffering was real, but there was no experience of pain. Christ, according to Hilary, "felt the force of passion, but without its pain" (*Adferrent quidem haec impetum passionis, non tamen dolorem passionis inferrent*).[16]

> [As] a dart passing through water, or piercing a flame, or wounding the air, inflicts all that it is its nature to do: it passes through, it pierces, it wounds; but all this is without effect on the thing it strikes; since it is against the order of nature to make a hole in water, or pierce flame, or wound

---

16   Hilary of Poitiers, *De Trinitate* X, 23. Cf. J. Mercer, "Suffering for our Sake: Christ and Human Destiny in Hilary of Poitiers's *De Trinitate*," in *Journal of Early Christian Studies* 22 (2014), 541-68.

the air, though it is the nature of a dart to make holes, to pierce and to wound.[17]

The reason, he argued, was the particular nature of Christ's human body. After all, Hilary suggested, Christ was able to walk on water and pass through walls, both of which were impossible for normal human beings; it was therefore legitimate to deduce that he experienced his crucifixion differently from what the same would have meant for others.

Throughout the Middle Ages, authors for whom Hilary was an authority grappled with the task of explaining the reality and limits of Christ's psychological experience in his suffering. In this attempt, they drew mainly on Augustine and John of Damascus, whose stance was at variance with Hilary's. Both Patristic authorities acknowledged the reality of Jesus' "feelings of weakness" (Augustine[18]) and indeed his participation in all human affections (Damascene[19]), but also gave clear indications that an unbridled affirmation of Christ's suffering was problematic because it could endanger divine impassibility. Thus Augustine opined that Christ "exercised these passions when he judged they should be exercised"; he

---

17   Hilary of Poitiers, *De Trinitate* X, 23; English translation from *Nicene and Post-Nicene Fathers* II, 9, 187–88.

18   Augustine, *Enarrationes in Psalmos* 87, 3.

19   John of Damascus, *De fide orthodoxa* III, 20.

experienced them only "when it pleased him."[20] And
John of Damascus read Jesus' cry of dereliction on
the cross ("My God, my God, why have thou forsak-
en me?") as appropriating the experience of humanity as a whole rather than representing his own.[21]

Medieval authors largely adopted the arguments
of Augustine (Peter Lombard[22]) or John of Damascus (Aquinas[23]) but acknowledged Hilary's weight as
an authority.[24] In this trajectory, Luther can be seen
as standing at the extreme end of a development
that led from Hilary's viewpoint, according to which
Christ's humanity did not permit the experience of
pain, to qualifications of this premise, and finally
reaching a position that accepted Christ's human
suffering as the starting point of any Christological
reflection.

The key text to be considered is Luther's exegesis
of Psalm 22 in his *Commentary on the Psalms* (*Operationes in Psalmos*) from 1519-1521.[25] Yet it is worthwhile recalling briefly an even earlier text, Luther's

---

20   Augustine, *De civitate Dei* XIV, 9.

21   John of Damascus, *De fide orthodoxa* III, 24.

22   Gondreau, *The Passions of Christ's Soul*, 58.

23   Ibid.

24   Ibid., 50–51.

25   On Luther's exegesis of this psalm, cf. also the com-
     prehensive study by Jens Wolff, *Metapher und Kreuz:
     Studien zu Luthers Christusbild* (Tübingen: Mohr
     Siebeck, 2005).

so-called *First Commentary on Psalms* (*Dictata super Psalterium*) from 1513. In these lectures, given four years prior to Luther's publication of his ninety-five theses, his specific hermeneutical and theological approach to the biblical text is already taking shape.

Luther follows a long-standing tradition of reading the Psalms christologically, whose ultimate authority was the New Testament.[26] Unsurprisingly perhaps, the main influence on Luther, the Augustinian friar, was the Bishop of Hippo himself; his *Enarrationes in Psalmos* were perhaps the single most influential Patristic exegetical text throughout the Middle Ages. But while Luther quotes Augustine at least 270 times in his lectures,[27] a change of emphasis is evident nonetheless. For Augustine, and the medieval tradition following him, the Christological reading of this biblical book was essentially inscribed into a vision of the "whole Christ" (*totus Christus*) comprising both Christ as the "head" (*caput*), that is the person of the savior himself, and as the "body" (*corpus*), the Church.[28] In practice, this meant that passages

---

26   Erich Vogelsang, *Die Anfänge von Luthers Christologie: Nach der ersten Psalmenvorlesung* (Berlin: de Gruyter, 1929), 17–18.

27   Friedrich Held, *Augustins Enarrationes in Psalmos als exegetische Vorlage für Luthers erste Psalmenvorlesung* (Gotha: Perthes, 1930), 17, quoted from Lienhard, *Martin Luthers Christologisches Zeugnis*, 20.

28   Cf. Augustine, *Enarrationes in Psalmos* 30, II, 3; Vogelsang, *Die Anfänge von Luthers Christologie*, 19.

within the Psalms that emphasized individual sinfulness or even individual suffering were ascribed to
affections of the Church in order to avoid inappro-
priate notions about the person of the savior.

Luther did not dispute the concept of the *totus
Christus* as such, but key for his concept of Christological exegesis even at this early point was 1 Corinthians 2, 2: "For I decided to know nothing among
you except Jesus Christ, and him crucified."[29] In
other words, it is the passion, and it is the cross, that
provides the necessary lens for understanding who
Jesus Christ was and who he was for his Church. As
a result, the Psalms of individual lament, which for
Augustine and other previous exegetes had seemed
a dangerous stumbling block insofar as they could
appear to impinge on Christ's full divinity, became
particularly important for Luther's theology even in
this early phase of his career. At the same time, this
reference to the cross makes it clear that Luther's interest in Christ's suffering had nothing to do with a
morbid fascination with his wounds, his pain, or his
blood. It gained its significance from the salvific im-
port Christ's death had for the believer. Christ's suffering had to be emphasized in the interest of a full
understanding of him as the savior. If Christology
was fundamental for Luther's thought, the reformer
never considered Christological questions abstract-
ed from their soteriological relevance.

29   WA 3, 13, 2; Vogelsang *Die Anfänge von Luthers
     Christologie*, 23.

It is this soteriological cast of his Christology that led him to seek out those passages in the Psalms that spoke of individual suffering, not merely physical, but mental and spiritual. For Luther, affirming Christ's true human suffering in the passion meant to take seriously those texts that spoke of his agony; his fear of dying; even his sense of alienation from God.

For these reasons, Luther was keen, in his *Operationes in Psalmos* (1519-1521), to identify the voice of Christ even in the Psalms of individual lament such as, famously, Psalm 22. "The cross alone," he says in these lectures, "is our theology."[30]

He explicitly criticized Church Fathers, even Augustine, for their refusal to apply certain verses to Christ's own experience and instead aimed to apply the whole psalm like a frame to his person (*omnia in propriam personam volo quadrare*).[31] For Luther, Christ did not merely suffer in his body but in his soul as well, thus identifying with human angst, with despair, and even with a sense of alienation from God. Christ in his passion really was afflicted; he experienced the pangs of divine wrath as much as any human being could ever feel them:

> The strikes of God with which he [sc. Christ] is struck for our sins are not only the pain of death but also the anxiety and the horror of an afflicted conscience that feels the eternal wrath and acts

---

30   WA 5, 176, 32.

31   WA 5, 610, 20.

> as if it were forsaken and expelled from his face
> forever.[32]

Christ was "forsaken by God" (*derelictum a deo*),[33] and "carried within himself God's wrath on our behalf" (*portans in seipso iram patris pro nobis*).[34]

We can say, Luther explains elsewhere, that Christ "was made sin for us" (cf. 2 Cor 5, 21) because

> ... deserted by God, without sin, he became similar
> in all things to the worst sinner whose conscience
> is only touched, and forced into desperation, by
> the wrath of God.[35]

Texts like this can be cited at length from the second Psalm Commentary. They indicate how radical Luther's emphasis on the parallel between Christ's suffering and human suffering was. Those undergoing spiritual trials (*Anfechtungen*) which, as Luther himself knew too well, include the experience of God as wrathful or distant can trust that Jesus knew what they were going through.

All this, however, Luther emphasizes, was part of God's salvific plan. Christ, he insists, was conceived by the Holy Spirit in the Virgin Mary "without sin," but

---

32　WA 5, 603, 14.

33　WA 5, 237, 38.

34　WA 5, 271, 25.

35　WA 5, 607, 31.

> ... at the time of his suffering, he accepted all our
> properties, which thus by exchange became his,
> and suffered for those things that we ought to
> have suffered.[36]

Luther was therefore careful not to cross the boundary that radically differentiates Christ's response to
these trials from ours. The reformer is entirely clear
that in spite of his temptations and trials Jesus himself was himself free from sin. Luther remarks that
it would be impossible for any sinful human being
to pray Psalm 22, 1 without blaspheming because
in our mouth, the cry "My God, why have you forsaken me" inevitably implies the suppression of our
awareness that God would be justified in forsaking
us. It would therefore always carry the notion of anger against, or even hatred of, God. It takes the sinless, the innocent Jesus to be able to say these words
"without blasphemy or grumbling."[37]

Luther's theology at this point, as so often, turns
on paradox: Jesus, the one human being in whom
God was uniquely present, experiences the radical
depth of God-forsakenness in order that humankind, which in reality is alienated and distant from
God, can again be reconciled with its creator. While
therefore Luther's emphasis on the reality of Christ's
human suffering is radical and uncompromising,
it does not mean that it can be detached from two

---

36   WA 5, 603, 7–10.

37   WA 5, 604, 28–30.

other aspects that characterize his Christology: encountering Christ as the suffering human being is inseparable from the encounter with Christ as God Incarnate; and the focus on the cross as the place where human sin is overcome is inseparable from its orientation towards the ultimate victory over death in the resurrection.

2 Encountering God in Christ

Luther's emphasis on the reality of Christ's human experience did not mean that Jesus for him was primarily a human being. On the contrary, he believed that Christian faith in its entirety depended on the truth that in Jesus Christ we truly encounter God (cf. Col. 2, 9) and that everything that happened to the savior can also be said to have affected God as well.[38] If his affirmation of Christ's human agony was radical, his insistence that in this man, and only in him, God revealed himself fully was equally radical and, once again, driven by the uncompromising emphasis of his theology on human salvation.

In order to explain more fully how Christology for Luther required that it is truly God whom we encounter in Jesus Christ, but also how this emphasis on Christ's divinity was part of his overall, distinctive Christological vision, I will first comment on Luther's so-called theology of the cross, which is

---

38 Cf. LW 34, 207.

often credited as perhaps the major methodological basis of Luther's thought, but which is ultimately an attempt to discover the theological significance of God's presence in Christ's suffering on the cross. In a second step, I shall connect Luther's ideas with theological developments of the patristic period, in particular the emergence of the so-called theopaschite formula.

2.1 Theology of the Cross

Until the early twentieth century, Luther's theology of the cross (*theologia crucis*) was routinely considered marginal to Luther's thought or even as belonging to his monastic, pre-Reformation period. Things changed radically, however, with Walther von Loewenich's 1929 study on the subject,[39] and ever since the idea has found widespread acceptance that the theology of the cross embodies the core of Luther's Christocentric theory of revelation.

---

39   Walther von Loewenich, *Luthers Theologia Crucis* (4th ed.; Munich: Kaiser, 1954); cf. Alister McGrath, *Luther's Theology of the Cross: Martin Luther's Theological Breakthrough*, 2nd ed. (Oxford: Wiley-Blackwell, 2011); Robert C. Saler, "The Cross and the Theologia Crucis," in *Oxford Research Encyclopedia of Religion* [http://religion.oxfordre.com/view/10.1093/acrefore/9780199340378.001.0001/acrefore-9780199340378-e-340].

Its classical expression is to be found in the *Heidelberg Disputation* of 1518.[40] This important document of Luther's early theology offers a radically critical engagement with the scholastic theology of his academic teachers, notably Gabriel Biel. Scholastic theology, or what Luther considered under this epithet, represented to the reformer a thoroughly wrongheaded attempt to reflect on the Christian faith. Luther calls this a "theology of glory." This theology, he charges, "calls evil good and good evil." What is wrong with the theology of glory can, perhaps, become clearer by juxtaposing it with its opposite, the "theology of the cross," which "calls the thing what it is" (Th. 21).[41]

The task of theology, Luther argues, is missed where the "invisible" things of God are looked upon as though they were "clearly perceptible" (Th. 19).[42] Instead, God reveals himself "through suffering and the cross," and it is there that the true theologian must seek him (Th. 20).[43] Luther's point, in other words, is that true theology will be cautious towards a knowledge of God that is gained from what in his creation seems most evidently to point to him. Perhaps it is too strong to call him an early critic of natural theology, but he certainly puts up a warning

---

40   LW 31, 35–70.

41   LW 31, 40.

42   LW 31, 40.

43   LW 31, 40.

sign against attempts of this kind. His reason is not that such knowledge is in principle impossible, but that under the conditions of sin it inevitably is fed by the wrong reasons and motivations. It is a theology detached from any concern about human fallenness and human need for salvation. It is *therefore* a theology inspired by pride and an abstraction from human sinfulness that is in itself sinful.

To appreciate Luther's harsh binary, we may recall St Paul's insistent questioning of the fact that God chose to reveal himself through the cross. "We proclaim Christ crucified, a stumbling-block to Jews and foolishness to Gentiles," he wrote to the Corinthians (1 Cor 1, 23). And in Galatians he observed that Christ "redeemed us from the curse of the law by becoming a curse for us – for it is written, 'Cursed is everyone who hangs on a tree'" (Gal 3, 13). Given that the cross is a stumbling block, it must be explained. Luther's explanation is that only such a revelation *per passionem et crucem*, through passion and the cross, permits a human encounter with God that is not endangered by the human tendency to equate oneself with God (cf. Gen 3,5) but instead opens the eyes to the need, and the promise, of salvation.

The idea that God must be found hidden from sight was not Luther's own discovery. Luther encountered it as part of the Platonic tradition within Christian theology chiefly connected with the anonymous author known as pseudo-Dionysius the Areopagite. In his *First Psalms Commentary*, Luther explains Psalm 18, 11 ("The hiding place of God is darkness") with a direct reference to "blessed Dionysius" who taught to "enter into anagogical darkness and ascend by way of denials."[44] Yet he goes on to emphasize another kind of "darkness," namely that of Christ's humanity in his Incarnation: "He is concealed in humanity, which is His darkness. Here He could not be seen but only heard" (*in humanitatem absconditus latet, que est tenebre eius, in quibus videri not potuit sed tantum audiri*).[45]

Luther scholars have debated whether passages like this prove Luther's debt to the Platonic tradition and, in particular, its flourishing in late medieval German mysticism, or whether they give evidence of Luther's decisive break with this tradition.[46] More important than an adjudication of the question of historical genealogy, however, is the theological significance of Luther's own position. Luther's theology of the cross is, first of all, a kind of theological epistemology; it suggests a privileged way of approaching God through a revelation that seems intuitively the exact opposite of divine reality: humiliation, pain,

---

44   WA 3, 124, 29ff.

45   English translation in LW 10, 120.

46   On the complex relationship of Luther and mysticism see Bernd Hamm, "How Mystical Was Luther's Faith?" in *The Early Luther: Stages in a Reformation Reorientation*, by Bernd Hamm, trans. Martin J. Lohrmann (Grand Rapids, MI: Eerdmans, 2010), 190–231.

lowliness, suffering, defeat, and death. Yet underlying this epistemological thesis is a religious and ultimately an existential attitude. Luther demands that God must be approached in the lowliness of Christ's Incarnation rather than in the seemingly apparent glory of his historical actions, because only the former is compatible with human faith in God's grace. Since human beings are lost without grace, the alternative between the theology of the cross and the theology of glory is not just an alternative between right and wrong opinion but ultimately one between damnation and salvation.[47]

There is another aspect to this argument. As we have seen, earlier Christian authors were concerned that the reality of Christ's suffering could lead to the denial of his full divinity. The theology of the cross, we can now see, is the key that allowed Luther to be dismissive about such qualms. The Incarnation in lowliness, and particularly the cross, he held, was not even potentially a blemish on God's glory, but rather the proper way Christ's being is revealed to human beings under the condition of sin. Human beings must not search for God elsewhere; he shows himself *sub contrario specie*, hidden in suffering humanity. "He who does not know Christ, does not know God in suffering" (Proof of Th. 21).[48]

Luther's biblical basis for this theory subtly ties together three separate but equally important scrip-

---

47   LW 31, 53.

48   LW 31, 53.

tural texts. Firstly, there is the notion of the "hidden God" as expressed by the Second Isaiah (Is 45, 15): "Truly, you are a God who hides himself, O God of Israel, the Savior." Secondly, as we have already seen, Luther relies on St. Paul and especially his injunction against the "wisdom of this world" in 1 Corinthians (1 Cor 1, 18-31). A third aspect, which is sometimes overlooked but is absolutely central is Luther's debt to the Christology of the Gospel of John with its insistence that those who encounter Jesus encounter truly and fully God. One of Luther's favourite New Testament verses is therefore John 14, 8, in which Jesus assures Philip that "He who has seen me has seen the Father." The theology of the cross weaves these three complex biblical notions into a paradoxical conjunction of opposites: the supreme God is recognized in his abasement, and the virtuous one in his exposure to evil; the omnipotent being is found in utter weakness.[49]

Luther's insistence on the reality of Christ's human experience, then, had nothing to do with a reduction of Christ to a purely or largely human Jesus. Instead, the weakness of the suffering Jesus becomes the exclusive locus in which the almighty God has chosen to approach sinful humanity. Jesus therefore is fully divine; but in and through him, God also became fully and truly human. As much as it is the case, according to Luther, that he who sees the Son sees the Father, as much is it also true and inevitable

---

49   LW 31, 52–53.

that we encounter God *in* this human being: "Whoever does not find or receive God in Christ shall nevermore and nowhere have or find God outside of Christ, even though he should go beyond heaven, below hell, or outside of the world."[50]

With this use of paradoxical language to describe the reality of God's revelation in and through Jesus Christ, especially in and through his suffering on the cross, Luther harks back to some of the earliest Christian texts dealing with the Incarnation. At the end of the first century, Ignatius of Antioch called Jesus "both made and not made; God existing in flesh; true life in death; both of Mary and of God; first passible and then impassible."[51] Melito of Sardis (died *ca.* 180) employed even more strikingly paradoxical language in his famous *Paschal Homily*:

> The one who hung the earth in space, is himself hanged; the one who fixed the heavens in place, is himself impaled; the one who firmly fixed all things, is himself firmly fixed to the tree. The Lord is insulted; God has been murdered ...[52]

This debt Luther's theology of the cross owes to the earliest Christian tradition must not be ignored; it would nevertheless be facile simply to identify the two. In its entirety, Luther's concept is a novel contribution to the history of Christian thought albeit

---

50   LW 34, 207.

51   Ignatius of Antioch, *Epistle to the Ephesians* 7, 2.

52   Melito of Sardis, *Paschal Homily* 96.

with roots in earlier thought. For Luther as for the early Fathers, the recognition of God in the lowliness of Jesus' humanity, in the passion and on the cross, is wondrous and evidence of God's might and love, but to the reformer it also indicates the enormous power that sin, death, and the devil have in the world, such that they could be overcome only in this particular manner. Human beings, Luther insists, are so deeply implicated in this fallenness of creation that *any* attempt to approach God through the theology of glory falls foul of their sinful tendency of self-justification and self-aggrandizement. More abstractly, Luther's theology of the cross represents, and is faithful to, the overall, radically soteriological cast of his thought. Neither God's incarnation nor his revelation can be properly understood apart from his intention to save the world, and apart from the world's need to be saved.

2.2 The Theopaschite Formula

If Christ's suffering is key for human salvation, and if God specifically reveals himself in and through the lowliness of this experience, the question arises of whether and how it can be said that God suffers on the cross. For Luther, it was of crucial importance that the passion was not only that of a human being, since no such suffering could be salvific: "For if I believe that only the human nature suffered for me, then Christ would be a poor Savior for me, in fact, he himself would need a Savior."[53] Luther has therefore often been seen as a forerunner of theologies of the suffering God, for better or worse.[54]

It is, however, doubtful that such a characterization is ultimately helpful. Luther stood in the tradition of early Christian authors such as Melito ("God has been murdered"), whose intent was not to predicate suffering of God but to emphasize the unity of the divine and human in the person of Christ. In Christ, God became human, and everything, therefore, that was true of humanity could also be said of God. Equally, everything that was true of the Godhead could be said of the human person, Jesus. Not only did this view not require a suffering divinity; on the contrary, the paradoxical character of the Christ event would arguably be lost if the divinity itself was *like* humanity. If there was nothing unusual about God's suffering, there would be no need to emphasize the uniqueness of the Incarnation and its basis in God's loving and salvific will. As it is, two utterly distinct and different beings, divine and human, became one person in such a way that no separation

---

53   LW 37, 210.

54   Thomas Weinandy, *Does God Change? The Word's Becoming in the Incarnation* (Still River, MA: St. Bede's Publications, 1985), 101–108.

between them was conceivable, even though each also remained what it was.[55]

In precisely the same sense, Cyril of Alexandria included denial of divine suffering in the flesh in his anathemas against Nestorius:

> Whosoever shall not recognize that the Word of God suffered in the flesh, that he was crucified in the flesh, and that likewise in that same flesh he tasted death and that he is become the first-begotten of the dead, for, as he is God, he is the life and it is he that giveth life: let him be anathema.[56]

Nestorius had been insistent on the need to preserve the respective characteristics of the two natures even in the Incarnation. His interest was to ensure that both, the full divinity *and* the full humanity of the savior were kept intact, not one at the expense of the other. Yet his Alexandrian opponent became increasingly concerned that in this way the close and intimate – Cyril would influentially say "hypostatic" – union of the two in the person of Jesus Christ could not be preserved, and without that union, there was no salvation. For Cyril, as for Irenaeus and Athanasius, the Incarnation was summed up by John 1, 14: "the Word became Flesh"; if that required the use of

---

55   Cf. WA 39/II:101,15–16: *Ab aeterno non est passus, sed cum factus est homo, est passibilis.*

56   Cyril of Alexandria, *Epistula II Ad Nestorium* (ACO [*Acta Conciliorum Oecumenicorum*] I, 1, 1, 42, 2–5).

paradox, then paradox had to be used. Prescribing the language of divine suffering "in the flesh," Cyril was evidently careful to exclude a violation of divine impassibility: God suffered, we might paraphrase, *only* in the flesh. Yet if this qualification was important, it was nonetheless equally significant that it was *God* who truly suffered in the flesh.

Cyril's insistence on divine suffering in the Incarnation was subsequently seen as a major aspect of his teaching that had to be integrated into the language of Chalcedon to stem a potential Nestorian interpretation of the Council's emphasis on the two natures in the one person of Jesus Christ and thus to ensure that the Council would find universal acceptance. This was the subject of the so-called theopaschite controversy which continued for several decades in the former half of the sixth century.[57] The central focus of this controversy was the doctrinal formula that "one of the Holy Trinity was crucified" (*unus ex sancta trinitate crucifixus est*). The formula itself was apparently first used by Patriarch Proclus of Constantinople in the late fifth century,[58] but while it is not found anywhere in Cyril's extant works, it is easy to see how it could be seen as naturally following from his twelfth anathema against Nestorius.

---

57   Aloys Grillmeier/Theresia Hainthaler, *Jesus der Christus im Glauben der Kirche*, vol. II/2: *Die Kirche von Konstantinopel im sechsten Jahrhundert* (Freiburg: Herder, 1989), 333-59.

58   Ibid. 334–35.

The formula of course was *not* meant to suggest that "God suffered"; the term "theopaschite" is misleading and was, unsurprisingly, coined by those who opposed it. The purpose of those propagating its inclusion into the Church's dogmatic vocabulary, chiefly a group of monks from Scythia, the area near the estuary of the Danube, was to ensure the continuity between the second Person of the Trinity, the divine Logos, and the Person of the Incarnate throughout his entire earthly life. The paradoxical "theopaschite" language, identifying God himself with human weakness and suffering, was a price to be paid, as it were, to ensure this identity.

Nevertheless, there was resistance against the use of such language, and nowhere more than in Rome. It was the theologically minded Emperor of Byzantium, Justinian I, who made the theopaschite position his own and, after more than a decade of ceaseless pleading ensured its acceptance by both East and West. Eventually, the theopaschite formula was included in Justinian's great ecclesiastical triumph, the Fifth Ecumenical Council of 553.[59] Yet its use by many Patristic and medieval authors was so guarded against the potential implication that God was passible that the Christological potential contained in the idea that in Christ God *truly* suffered in the flesh was often lost.[60]

---

59   Canon X (ACO IV, 1, 218).

60   Oswald Bayer, "Das Wort ward Fleisch: Luthers Christologie als Lehre von der Idiomenkommunika-

Luther's position can therefore, in one sense, be described as an attempt to recover the full, subversive potential of theopaschite language. First of all, he is clear that it is not "divinity" that suffers, but God united with humanity in the incarnation. Thus he wrote in his controversy with Zwingli:

> You must say that the person (pointing to Christ) suffers, and dies. But this person is truly God, and therefore it is correct to say: the Son of God suffers. Although, so to speak, the one part (namely, the divinity) does not suffer, nevertheless the person, who is God, suffers in the other part (namely, in the humanity).[61]

Nevertheless, there is no denying that Luther's use of the theopaschite formula went further than did the previous tradition. He was less concerned by its potential to vitiate the notion of God's impassibility than Patristic and medieval authorities had generally been, as is clear, for example, from his willingness fully to embrace the theological consequences of Jesus' cry of dereliction (Mt. 27, 46).[62] Yes, God suf-

---

tion," in *Creator est Creatura: Luthers Christologie als Lehre von der Idiomenkommunikation*, ed. by Oswald Bayer and Benjamin Gleede (Berlin/New York: de Gruyter, 2007), 5–34, here 13. Cf. Werner Elert, "Die theopaschitische Formel," *Theologische Literaturzeitung* 4/5 (1950), 44–55.

61 LW 37, 210.

62 Lienhard, *Martin Luthers Christologisches Zeugnis*, 90.

fered "only" in the flesh, but he really *suffered* in the flesh. Unless both sides of the paradox were equally emphasized, the full truth of Christology was not preserved. Undoubtedly, this tendency derived once again from Luther's soteriological approach to Christology; in fact, Werner Elert saw the very purpose of the theopaschite formula in its alignment of the soteriological and the Christological perspectives.[63]

This radically soteriological approach to Christology has sometimes been fastened on by critics of Luther's teaching as evidence that his theology as a whole is one-sided and therefore ultimately untenable. It has led him, according to these critics, both to a flawed doctrine of a passible God and to an unsatisfactory Christology. Such critics, however, take for granted what may be called a metaphysical approach to theology. In such an understanding of the task of the theologian, philosophical assumptions about, for example, the properties of God or of human nature will inevitably be prioritized and determine the shape of Christian doctrine as a whole. Narrow limits are consequently put on the language of "divine suffering."

Luther, however, has a radically different conception of the theologian's job, as we have already seen in discussing his theology of the cross. Unsurprisingly, he has therefore been accused of anti-philosophical hostility – a charge which, in fairness, he himself has courted by frequent invectives against "the philoso-

---

63   Elert, "Die theopaschitische Formel," 200.

phers." Such a charge is, nonetheless, misguided or at least misleading. His position is not anti-philosophical, but feeds from the legitimate concern that abstract, metaphysical reflection may well come to its limits when fundamental, existential and personal issues are at stake. Far from being anti-philosophical, Luther arguably stands at the origin of some of the most powerful philosophical insights developed in the modern period.[64]

3 Encountering the Victorious Christ

If Luther in his view of God's suffering often went further than the tradition, it is equally noticeable that he stood apart from the late medieval fascination with the human suffering of Christ as such, let alone the idea that Christian existence should consist in the imitation of Christ's passion.[65] Instead, just as Cyril in his twelfth anathema had insisted that "the Word of God suffered in the flesh … and *that he is become the first-begotten of the dead,*" so Luther too was adamant in his affirmation of the con-

64   Simon D. Podmore, "Luther in Modern European Philosophy," in *Oxford Research Encyclopedia of Religion* [http://religion.oxfordre.com/view/10.1093/acrefore/9780199340378.001.0001/acrefore-9780199340378-e-317].

65   Uwe Rieske-Braun, *Duellum mirabile: Studien zum Kampfmotiv in Martin Luthers Theologie* (Göttingen: Vandenhoeck & Ruprecht, 1999), 100–103.

nection between Christ's death and his resurrection. After all, the importance of God's presence on the cross was that this particular death led to victory over death, sin, and the devil. Luther never neglected the insight that the paradoxical lowliness of God in the incarnation ultimately led not to the abasement of God but to the glorification of humanity. Good Friday and Easter for him belonged together in the drama of human salvation.

It is at this point that we need to consider somewhat more closely Luther's theory of atonement. As much as we have found that his Christology is focused on salvation, however, his understanding of salvation is inextricably intertwined with his view of the person of Christ as well. Reflections on Luther's soteriology will therefore ultimately lead back to a deepened understanding of his Christology.

3.1 Luther's Understanding of the Atonement

To those familiar with the emphasis in contemporary evangelical theology on penal substitution, it may come as a surprise that there is even a debate about Luther's theory of the atonement. It is indeed easy to get the impression that, many disagreements in detail within the Protestant tradition notwithstanding, there is unanimity on this: that Christ brought salvation to humankind by vicariously taking on himself the punishment that humanity had incurred by disobeying the divine command.[66] Christ's death on the cross, on this reading, is the single act that reconciles God and humankind, stilling the wrath of God on the basis of a perfect as well as innocent sacrifice that could only be offered by God Incarnate himself.

There can be but little doubt that this theory has been espoused by the confessional documents on which mainstream Protestant churches have based their identities, and it has certainly dominated doctrinal solidification during the subsequent, so-called orthodox phase of Lutheran as well as Calvinist theology from the sixteenth to the early eighteenth centuries. Yet as soon as historical scholarship began to discern that Luther's teaching was often not simply identical with the dogmatics of later orthodoxy, readers of his works could not help observing that the evidence for Luther's adherence to the penal substitution model was, if anything, messy; in fact, many have concluded that it is altogether misleading to count him as a representative of this view.[67]

---

66   Cf. Darren W. Snyder Belousek, *Atonement, Justice, and Peace: The Message of the Cross and the Mission of the Church* (Grand Rapids, MI: Eerdmans, 2012), 83–94. Ibid., 83: "The dominant understanding of the death of Jesus within Evangelical Protestant Christianity is the doctrine of penal substitution atonement."

67   Cf. the overview in Matthieu Arnold, "Luther on Christ's Person and Work," in Robert Kolb/Irene Dingel/L'ubomír Batka (eds.), *The Oxford Handbook of Martin Luther's Theology* (Oxford: Oxford University Press, 2014), 274-75.

At first sight, admittedly, this seems counterintuitive. Has not even the brief and inevitably superficial overview of some aspects of Luther's Christological thought given heretofore exhaustively documented Luther's central concern with the cross, arguably to the point of obsession? Did the reformer not, in characteristically hyperbolic language, profess that "the cross is our theology?" Clearly then his soteriology must be strongly focussed on Christ's death on the cross as well?

The centrality of the cross in Luther's theology can indeed not be doubted. But as we have seen also, the cross for the reformer was much more than shorthand for Christ's salvific death. Rather, one could say that it symbolizes the paradoxical truth that human beings come closest to God in the one place that is seemingly most remote from him. In this sense, the theology of the cross was much more than a reflection on the atoning death of Christ; it was a theory of revelation and, ultimately, a summary of Luther's theological hermeneutic.

Again, when Luther identified "the cross" with his "whole theology," he arguably did not think of a transactional moment of human delivery from God's righteous wrath. It would be more appropriate to say that the cross for Luther represents the climax of the Incarnation; it is the single moment that exemplifies most distinctly what the whole of the Incarnation signifies: in order to save humankind, God revealed himself "concealed in humanity, which is his dark-

ness" (WA 3, 124, 34-35); it is for this reason that
he can only be known "in passion and in the cross"
as Luther argued in the *Heidelberg Disputation*.
Reading Luther's language of the centrality of the
cross along those lines, the meaning of his emphasis on the cross in his account of human salvation
does no longer seem like a foregone conclusion. On
the contrary, once the reader of Luther's sprawling
oeuvre has been alerted to this issue, one can hardly
overlook the many texts in which the reformer es-
pouses a view of Christ's salvific work that is starkly
at variance with the substitutionary theory of atonement that is usually traced back to Anselm of Canterbury's treatise *Why God Became Man* and which
foregrounds the need for God's righteousness to be
restored by means of a perfect as well as innocent
sacrificial offering.

Instead, Luther speaks of the atonement in the
dramatic metaphors of a battle between God and
the opposing evil forces – sin, death, and the devil –
from which Christ emerges victorious at Easter. Ultimately, without taking away the focus on the cross
and on Good Friday, this view of salvation finds its
fulfilment in the resurrection of Christ. Vivid and
powerful expressions of this soteriological conception underlie some of Luther's most well-known
poetic texts.

In his Easter hymn "Death Held our Lord in Pris-
on" (*Christ lag in Todesbanden*), for example, Easter
is presented as the outcome of a struggle between

Jesus Christ and the opposing powers, sin, devil, and death, who previously "held us all in his kingdom." "All sons of men were helpless" in the face of these forces because death was the result of sin, and "no one was yet guiltless." Christ's Incarnation is seen in this context; he is the one who brings victory, but only after he had been given over to death "for our offenses":

> Jesus Christ, God's only Son,
> Into our place descending,
> Away with [all] our sins hath done,
> And therewith from Death rending
> Right and might, made him a jape,
> Left him nothing but Death's shape:
> His ancient sting—he has lost it. Alleluia!
>
> That was a right wondrous strife
> When Death in Life's grip wallowed:
> Off victorious came Life,
> Death he has quite upswallowed.
> The Scripture has published that—
> How one Death the other ate.
> Thus Death is become a laughter. Alleluia![68]

Similarly, the hymn "Dear Christians, One and All Rejoice" (*Nun freut euch lieben Christen g'mein*) describes the Incarnation in these words: "Secret he bore his strength enorm, / He went about in my poor form, / For he would catch the devil."[69] Yet the

68   LW 53, 256–257.

69   LW 53, 220.

same language can be found across the whole range of Luther's writings, in biblical commentaries as well as in sermons, in polemical writings as much as in his Catechisms.

Given the presence of this theme even in all these texts, one wonders how they could ever have been overlooked. The answer is that the underlying theory of the atonement was for a long time not recognized in its theological significance, and Luther's use of the "stupendous duel" (*duellum mirabile*) was therefore not taken seriously as an important aspect of his theology. These texts were therefore often written off as part of Luther's tendency to plunder the language of the tradition in the interest of rhetorical and spiritual effect more than theological subtlety.

The person who has done more than anyone else to change this perception was the Swedish Lutheran theologian and bishop Gustaf Aulén. In his 1931 book *Christus Victor: An Historical Study of the Three Main Types of Atonement Theory*,[70] Aulén not only privileged Luther's use of the stupendous duel in his reconstruction of the reformer's theology, but argued that he had in fact recovered and improved what really was the "classical" view of the atonement. Aulén drew a direct line from early Church Fathers such as Irenaeus, Athanasius, and Gregory of Nyssa to the

---

70 Gustaf Aulén, *Christus Victor: An Historical Study of the Three Main Types of Atonement Theory*, trans. A. G. Hebert (London: SPCK, 1931). Cf. Rieske-Braun, *Duellum mirabile*, 52–57.

sixteenth century reformer. Rather than the survival of an almost pre-theological and quasi-mythological idea of salvation, the presence of what Aulén himself called the Christus Victor model in Luther's thought signified the rediscovery of the most ancient as well as theologically most promising view of the atonement.

The theological strength of the Christus Victor model compared to its competitors consisted, according to Aulén, in its recognition of God's activity and initiative throughout the salvific process. While the "Latin model," favored by Anselm of Canterbury, Western scholasticism as well as the Protestant divines of the seventeenth century, prioritized the legal equivalence of transgression and punishment and developed, therefore, increasingly complicated theories of intertwined divine and human agency in order to explain how God's justice can be restored by Christ's death on the cross, the Christus Victor model is firmly focused on God's redeeming agency out of his love for his creation. The same love that explains the Incarnation (John 3, 16) explains how "in Christ God was reconciling the world to himself" (2 Cor 5, 19). There is no need, then, for God to be propitiated; atonement and reconciliation mean one and the same thing: God and his creation, which have been estranged on account of sin and evil, are brought together again due to God's own redeeming will and agency.

It is arguable that in his attempt to inscribe Luther's view on the atonement into a grand arc reaching back to the early Church, but also forward into Aulén's own time, the Swedish theologian offered a somewhat one-sided picture of the reformer's thought. While the parallel he drew with the Greek Fathers chimes with other observations adduced in the course of this lecture and surely opens up a fruitful field of thinking about Luther's theology, critics have rightly pointed out the prevalence in Luther's thought of precisely the ideas Aulén was so strongly opposed to: Luther clearly speaks and writes about God's wrath, not only because this was an idea he found in the Bible but also because the drama of salvation, as he saw it, was inscribed into the dialectic of human sin and God's anger in its face.[71] And for all the early Patristic leanings in Luther's soteriology, his notion of sin follows the forensic logic of Pauline theology and the Western medieval, especially the later nominalist, tradition: sin is the violation of God's law, and its consequence, therefore, is the impending punishment by eternal damnation. Any account of the atonement, therefore, had to include an explanation of how God's righteousness could be restored. It could not, in other words, be only or mainly directed, as in most of the Greek Fathers, at overcoming human mortality and corruptibility, but had to be construed in legal and ethical categories as

---

71   E.g. WA 50, 471, 1–8. Cf. Rieske-Braun, *Duellum mirabile*, 192–95.

well. Hence the centrality for Luther of the doctrine
of justification!

Yet for Luther the solution to this problem lay,
once again, in a focus on Jesus Christ as divine gift
(*sacramentum*) to humankind, much more than
on the objective righteousness of the Father which
many medieval scholastics had emphasized in their
theories.[72] God's righteousness, of which Paul spoke
in Romans 1, 17, was ultimately human righteousness before God imputed to the believer through
Jesus Christ. God's wrath and his judgment must
be understood as God's strange work (*opus alienum*)
ordained towards his proper work (*opus proprium*),
salvation. In this sense, Luther's soteriology is thoroughly Christocentric.

3.2 *Yves Congar's Criticism of Luther's Christology*

Yves Congar, writing in 1951, reconstructed Luther's
Christology almost exactly along the lines of Aulén's
Christus Victor theory even though the Swedish
theologian does not seem to have exerted a major influence on Congar's interpretation.[73] Where the Lu-

---

72   Rieske-Braun, *Duellum mirabile*, 195–96.

73   Yves Congar, "Regards et réflexions sur la christolo-
     gie de Luther," in Aloys Grillmeier/Heinrich Bacht,
     Das Konzil von Chalkedon: Geschichte und Gegenwart, 3
     vols. (Würzburg: Echter, 1951), 3, 457–86; cf. the brief
     reference to "théologiens protestants suédois," ibid.,

theran theologian had found in Luther an account
of the atonement emphasizing God's uninterrupted
agency throughout the redemptive process, the great
Dominican diagnosed in the reformer a Christology based on God's "unique efficacy" or the "efficacy
of God alone" (*christologie de l'Alleinwirksamkeit
Gottes*[74]). Whereas, however, Aulén had considered
it a strength of the "classical theory" that it relied
on God's sole agency, Congar saw Luther fall back
behind an insight developed in Aquinas: a proper
Chalcedonian Christology in which not only divinity but humanity too had its role to play in bringing
about the salvific act.

Congar perceived here a crucial and ultimately
deeply problematical one-sidedness in the reformer's
thought. The conciliar theologian expressed considerable sympathies for the cause of the Reformation
and more specifically for Luther's insistence on God's
sovereignty against a form of Christianity overly reli-
ant on the power of salvation mediated by the saints,
the sacraments, the papacy, not least indulgences.[75]
In the end, however, he saw Luther's understandable and probably necessary reaction as falling into

---

468. On Congar's interpretation of Luther throughout
his work, cf. Paweł Pielka, "Le dialogue avec le protestantisme dans la théologie d'Yves Congar," *Studia Oecu-
menica* 12 (2012), 299–326.

74   Congar, "Regards et réflexions sur la christologie de
Luther," 468, 486.

75   Pielka, "Le dialogue avec le protestantisme," 301.

the opposite extreme leading to an interpretation of Christianity seriously upsetting the equilibrium of divine and human co-operation as ultimately underwritten by the formula of Chalcedon and developed by the subsequent, Catholic tradition.

In this sense, Congar adopted the charge that Luther's Christology was at its heart monophysite.[76] We shall have to come back to this problem; for the moment let it be noted that perhaps a better term for what Congar has in mind would be "monergetic," suggesting that the unity of the person of the savior is underwritten by one, single source of activity and agency. Monergetic Christology, confessing two natures but insisting on one single source of operation, was one of several seventh-century attempts to bring about reconciliation between the Chalcedonian and the miaphysite churches; it was ultimately rejected by the sixth Ecumenical Council in 680/1.[77] More importantly, however, the idea that Christ's divinity is the active principle in his divine-human person was an extremely popular one among the earlier Fathers.

In the fourth century, for example, we find Gregory of Nyssa explain the unity of divine and human

---

76   Congar, "Regards et réflexions sur la christologie de Luther," 485.

77   Cf. Christian Lange, *Mia Energeia: Untersuchungen zur Einigungspolitik des Kaisers Heraclius und des Patriarchen Sergius von Constantinopel* (Tübingen: Mohr Siebeck, 2012).

drawing on the Stoic notion of the "active" and the "passive" principle (τὸ ποῖον, τὸ πάσχον[78]):

> And we say that, inasmuch as the Son is God, he is of course impassible and pure, but if any suffering is attributed to him in the Gospel, he carried out such an act through the humanity, which was of course susceptible to suffering. The Godhead quite certainly carried out the salvation of the world through the body he wore, so that the suffering belonged to the flesh, the action to God.[79]

Here we have an illustration of what a "Christology of God's efficacy alone" looks like. If Christ is said to suffer, this is the passivity of the human nature on which the agency of the divine works. "The suffering (τὸ πάθος) belonged to the flesh, the action (ἐνέργεια) to God."

On the basis of this Christology, Gregory can elsewhere interpret the parable of the Good Samaritan in strikingly physical terms. The Samaritan, in his allegorical exegesis, is Christ, more precisely the Logos,

> … who wrapped the whole of humanity about him through the first fruits of the dough, in

---

78 *Stoicorum Veterum Fragmenta* I, 85 (p. 24, 5-8); English translation: A. A. Long/D. N. Sedley (eds.), *The Hellenistic Philosophers*, vol. 1 (Cambridge: Cambridge University Press, 1987), 268.

79 Gregory of Nyssa, *Contra Eunomium* III/4, 8-9 (*Gregorii Nysseni Opera* [GNO] 2, 136, 18-24).

which there was a portion of every nation, of
Jew and Samaritan and Greek and all human
beings at once.[80]

Here the passivity of human nature extends not
merely to the humanity of the savior himself but to
the entire race. They all become objects of salvation
by virtue of being infused with divinity following on
from the Incarnation.

These are, admittedly, extreme examples, but
they helpfully illustrate the limits of Congar's as-
cription to Luther of a Christology of "divine effect
alone." Why would we not find texts such as those
by Gregory of Nyssa in Luther? One answer surely
is that Luther's focus is fully on the divine-human
person of Jesus Christ, rather than on effects of either of the two natures. Yet there is a more specific
teaching to be considered as well, which can explain
why an interpretation such as Congar's is not ultimately convincing:[81] Luther's doctrine of the "joyful
exchange."

---

80   Gregory of Nyssa, *In Canticum Canticorum Hom-*
     iliae XIV (GNO VI, 427, 21 – 428, 2); English trans-
     lation: Norris, *Homilies on the Song of Songs* (Atlanta:
     Society of Biblical Literature, 2012), 453.

81   Note however that Congar explicitly lists the *ad-*
     mirabile commercium in support of his interpretation:
     "Regards et réflexions sur la christologie de Luther,"
     463–64.

3.3 The Christology of the Joyful Exchange

The joyful exchange or *admirabile commercium* is a theory that is classically expressed in Luther's 1520 writing *On Christian Freedom*, but found across all of his writings from his earliest theology. Some scholars have even sought to identify the idea as the intellectual center of Luther's theology.[82] It is closely connected with Luther's Christology but is also often described in conjunction with the reformer's use of the "stupendous duel."

At its heart, we find Luther's familiar soteriological focus. "Christ carries all our sin, and his righteousness is imparted to us in exchange" (*vicissim*), Luther observes in his early *Lectures on Romans*.[83] In Christ's redemptive work, he takes on himself all that separates human beings from God and in return gives to them all the blessings connected with God. One can easily recognize the paradoxical language so typical of the reformer's theology; its ultimate foundation is Luther's conviction that God reveals himself in the Incarnation hidden under human weakness in order to save humankind from sin. The language familiar from his theology of the cross is therefore to be found in the context of the joyful exchange as well: "God's foolishness and weakness before human beings are wisdom and virtue before God, while

---

82   Esp. Theobald Beer, *Der fröhliche Wechsel und Streit: Grundzüge der Theologie Martin Luthers*, 2 vols. (Leipzig: St. Benno, 1974).

83   WA 56, 267, 7.

the wisdom and the virtue of the world are foolishness and weakness, even death before God."[84]

The connection with the Christus Victor motif, but equally its Christological underpinning, becomes clearer in the context of *On Christian Freedom*. The argument in this treatise combines several strands: firstly, Luther describes human salvation in terms of the bridal metaphor that has been used by Christian writings since Origen's allegorical interpretation of the Song of Songs, albeit with a slight twist. It is faith, the reformer argues, that "unites the soul with Christ as a bride is united with her bridegroom" (LW 31, 351):

> Accordingly the believing soul can boast of and glory in whatever Christ has as though it were its own, and whatever the soul has Christ claims as his own. Let us compare these and we shall see inestimable benefits. Christ is full of grace, life, and salvation. The soul is full of sins, death, and damnation. Now let faith come between them and sins, death, and damnation will be Christ's, while grace, life, and salvation will be the soul's; for if Christ is a bridegroom, he must take upon himself the things which are his bride's and bestow upon her the things that are his. If he gives her his body and very self, how shall he not give her all that is his? And if he takes the body of the bride, how shall he not take all that is hers? (Ibid.)

---

84   WA 56, 173, 31–174, 2.

This union brings about an exchange of properties: "grace, life, and salvation" are given by Christ to the soul, whereas "sins, death, and damnation," which attain to the soul, are graciously accepted by the bridegroom, Christ.

In describing how this exchange becomes possible, secondly, Luther once again uses the language of the stupendous duel:

> Here we have a most pleasing vision not only of communion but of a blessed struggle and victory and salvation and redemption. Christ is God and man in one person. He has neither sinned nor died, and is not condemned, and he cannot sin, die, or be condemned; his righteousness, life, and salvation are unconquerable, eternal, omnipotent … Now since it was such a one who did all this, and death and hell could not swallow him up, these were necessarily swallowed up by him in a mighty duel; for his righteousness is greater than the sins of all men, his life stronger than death, his salvation more invincible than hell.[85]

Finally, the text is explicit about the Christological foundation of the stupendous duel that leads to the overcoming of sin and death: it is the coexistence in Christ of the two natures, divine and human. In the Latin version of the treatise, Luther uses remarkably technical language to emphasize this point which one might want to translate as "Christ is God and man in one and the same person" (*Christus sit deus*

---

85 LW 31, 351–52.

et homo eaque persona). It is this duality of natures
united in one person which enables human and ultimately cosmic redemption: Christ's sinless and immortal divinity takes on and defeats the vices and
the sins of humanity. Ultimately, Christ is victorious
because he is the God-man, but this takes nothing
away from the serious nature of the battle during
which he *really* is afflicted, anxious, and agonized.

It is true that the phrase "joyful exchange" or even
more the Latin *admirabile commercium* is misleading
insofar as it suggests a symmetric exchange between
two partners.[86] And it is also the case that Luther's
use of the mystical union between Christ and the
soul emphasizes faith alone on the side of the soul,
not imitation or any other religious activity. And yet
Luther's ideas as well as his language show distinctly
that Christ's humanity is not merely of secondary
interest as the passive recipient of divine agency, as
was the case in some Patristic texts. On the contrary,
Luther often comes close to a Christological language of symmetry between divine and human that
in some ways could be seen as vitiating against the
stronger emphasis on the divine nature as produc-
ing the single person of the savior on which the later
Chalcedonian tradition insisted.

We shall have to come back to this last point. So
much, however, seems evident: Luther's view of the
atonement firmly rests on his unitary Christology,

---

86   Lienhard, *Martin Luthers Christologisches Zeugnis*,
     107.

and references to Christ's two natures are therefore
foundational for its establishment. The dynamic of
the divine-human union in the savior is here given a
further dimension by being inscribed into the tem-
poral sequence of Good Friday and Easter. However
important the reality of divine and human suffering
may have been for Luther, the ultimate significance
of the incarnation is the outcome of that struggle,
the defeat of sin, death, and hell by virtue of Christ's
divine power.

***

This chapter has taken a somewhat oblique
approach to Luther's Christology. Faced with the
absence of a major Christological treatise, I have
chosen to rely on Luther's treatment of a range of related topics. Two observations may be most striking.
Firstly, those familiar with the doctrinal tradition
may have been surprised by the limited evidence of
technical Christology and the absence, by and large,
of the terminology that had become the hallmark of
Christological writing since the late Patristic period.
This absence is not complete; in fact, we will have to
delve somewhat more deeply into Luther's attempts
to relate his own insights to the language of the scholastic tradition. Yet it is the case that much can be
written about Luther's Christology without engag-
ing with the problems of the assumption of human
nature and its individuation, or the precise relationship between the two wills in the one person of the
savior.

At the same time, however, Luther's neglect of the technicalities of Christology does not mean that the doctrine of the person of Jesus Christ was unimportant to him. On the contrary, if this survey has shown anything, it might well be how closely Christological problems are interwoven with many of Luther's most celebrated contributions to the theological tradition; he himself is regularly emphatic in his insistence that his theories rest on a Christological foundation. Ultimately, neither his doctrine of justification nor his theology of the cross nor indeed his theory of the joyful exchange can be understood without taking into account Luther's underlying commitment to the doctrine of Christ's divine-human person. In sum, then, this chapter has confirmed that Luther's christocentrism (*solus Christus*) is tied together with an emphasis on Christology.

Can more be said about the specific shape Luther's Christology takes and why it does so? One advantage of starting from an examination of these non-technical discussions is that the connection between Luther's wider theological concerns and his Christological views comes directly into view. In other words, while the foregoing may not have furnished us with too much doctrinal detail, it permits to gauge rather well how the shape of Luther's Christology reflects the overall contours of his theological project.

As I have sought to demonstrate, this link between Luther's uncompromising demand to put Christ at the center of all theological thought and the specific character of Christological doctrine can be observed in three somewhat tensional theological tenets: Luther's emphasis on the radical affirmation of the identity of Christ's suffering with human suffering, physical as well as spiritual; his insistence that in this suffering we nevertheless encounter God and that this is, indeed, the only proper way for sinners to approach him; the firm focus on the victorious outcome of Christ's struggle with sin, death, and the devil, i.e., the connection between Good Friday and Easter.

More specifically for his Christology the following conclusions can provisionally be drawn. Firstly, we can easily see why Luther continually insists that the union of divine and human in Christ is the foundation of all his theology. None of the tenets examined above could be accounted for without a firm commitment to both Christ's divinity and his humanity.

Secondly, it has become clear that Luther's Christology owes much to the Alexandrian tradition and its insistence on the personal union of divine and human in Jesus Christ. In Luther's paradoxical statements about the revelation of God "hidden in humanity," his uncompromising use of the theopaschite formula as well as his idea of the joyful exchange are all outgrowth of a strongly unitary Christology.

Yet if this Alexandrian strand in Luther's Christology is sometimes so strongly emphasized that some have doubted its compatibility with Chalcedonian orthodoxy, there is a countervailing tendency as well.

Luther's Christology takes radically seriously the human reality of the Incarnate. In fact, as we have seen, the reformer is willing to set aside traditional qualms in connection with divine impassibility in the interest of a full embrace of Christ's experience as a human being in solidarity with ourselves.

3 LUTHER'S CHRISTOLOGY:
TRADITIONAL AND PROVOCATIVE

As we have seen on multiple occasions, Luther regularly affirmed that his teaching on the person of Jesus Christ was simply in line with the whole Catholic tradition as articulated by the Council of Chalcedon in 451. Jesus was fully divine and fully human, and while this union existed in a single person, the two natures came together "without confusion, without change, without division, without separation."[87] His readers, however, have not always agreed with this assessment but found that at closer inspection his views were hardly compatible with those enshrined in the teaching of the early Church.

The present chapter will seek to evaluate these conflicting claims. In addition to the topics that have been considered in the previous section, two further contexts will here be investigated in which Luther entered more deeply into the technicalities of the Christological problem: his controversy with Huldrych Zwingli about the Eucharist and his late, academic disputations about Christological topics. Immediately connected with these debates is Luther's understanding of the so-called communication of idioms, which is now often seen as the central theoretical notion underpinning his Christology

---

87   ACO II 1, 2, 102, 39.

with significance far beyond this particular doctrinal topic.

1 Luther and the Communication of Idioms

In his 1539 treatise *On the Councils and the Church*, Luther analyzed the doctrinal error of Nestorius, the Patriarch of Constantinople who was condemned at the Council of Ephesus in 431. Nestorius, Luther argued, did not deny Christ's humanity or his divinity. He did not even deny that the two natures became one person even though some have thought that. Still, Luther maintained, he was rightly condemned and indeed could have been condemned for much more than his refusal to confess that Mary was the "mother of God" (*theotokos*). For Nestorius would "not admit a *communicatio idiomatum*."[88] What is this communication of idioms?

> I cannot express that in one word in German. *Idioma* means that which is inherent in a nature or is its attribute, such as dying, suffering, weeping, speaking, laughing, eating, drinking, sleeping, sorrowing, rejoicing, being born, having a mother, suckling the breast, walking, standing, working, sitting, lying down, and other things of that kind, which are called *idiomata naturae humanae*, that is, qualities that belong to man by nature, which he can and must do or even suffer; for *idioma* in Greek, *proprium* in Latin, is a thing – let us, for

---

88   LW 41, 100.

the time being, call it an attribute. Again, an *idioma deitatis*, "an attribute of divine nature," is that it is immortal, omnipotent, infinite, not born, does not eat, drink, sleep, stand, walk, sorrow, weep – and what more can one say?[89]

What Nestorius denies, then, is not that "the carpenter Jesus was crucified and the same Jesus is the true God; what he denies is that "God was crucified by the Jews" because "crucifixion and death are *idiomata* or attributes not of divine but of human nature."[90]

The Christian teaching, by contrast, Luther describes in this way:

> We Christians must ascribe all the *idiomata* of the two natures of Christ … equally to him.[91] Consequently Christ is God and man in one person because whatever is said of him as man must also be said of him as God, namely, Christ has died, and Christ is God; therefore God died – not the separated God, but God united with humanity. For about the separated God both statements, namely, that Christ is God and that God died, are false; both are false, for then God is not man.[92]

The authority for this article of faith, according to the reformer, is Scripture itself: after all, the angel in

---

89   LW 41, 100-101.

90   LW 41, 101.

91   The text adds "both persons" but this must be an error.

92   LW 41, 103.

Lk 1, 32 announced to Mary that she would bear the
"son of *the most high*." Later in the same gospel, Eliza-
beth wondered "why has this happened to me, that
the mother of my Lord comes to me?" (Lk 1, 43); St
Paul wrote in Galatians that "God sent his Son, *born
of a woman*," and so forth. The Council then, Luther
suggested, merely confirmed what the authority of
Scripture had taught from the beginning.

Yet while Luther is indubitably right that Scriptural language was the origin of the doctrine of the
communication of idioms, it is nevertheless the case
that it took many centuries for the rule to emerge
and, as we shall see, its precise formulation is not
as clear-cut as Luther suggests. The conceptual development within the Greek church is succinctly
summed up by John of Damascus in the eighth century who writes as follows:

> When, then, we speak of His divinity we do not
> ascribe to it the properties of humanity. For we do
> not say that His divinity is subject to passion or
> created. Nor, again, do we predicate of His flesh
> or of His humanity the properties of divinity: for
> we do not say that His flesh or His humanity is
> uncreated. But when we speak of His subsistence,
> whether we give it a name implying both natures,
> or one that refers to only one of them, we still
> attribute to it the properties of both natures.
> For Christ, which name implies both natures, is
> spoken of as at once God and man ...; and when
> He is named Son of God and God, in reference
> to only one of His natures, He still keeps the

properties of the co-existing nature, that is, the flesh, being spoken of as God who suffers, and as the Lord of Glory crucified, not in respect of His being God but in respect of His being at the same time man … And this is the manner of the mutual communication, either nature giving in exchange to the other its own properties through the identity of the subsistence and the interpenetration of the parts with one another. Accordingly we can say of Christ: This our God was seen upon the earth and lived amongst men, and This man is uncreated and impassible and uncircumscribed.[93]

It is easy to recognize Luther's view in the Damascene's formulation, but it is equally simple to discern that things are more complicated than Luther in his admittedly popular writing intimated. Firstly, the main gist in Luther's comment is fully confirmed by John: due to the hypostatic or personal union of divine and human in the savior, it is appropriate to use divine and human predicates interchangeably as long as we speak of the single hypostasis. Secondly, however, there is also a limit to this practice. We are not allowed to apply human predicates to divine nature or *vice versa*. Luther had the same in mind when

---

93 John of Damascus, *On Orthodox Faith* III 4, English translation in *Nicene and Post-Nicene Fathers* II, 9, 49. Cf. Benjamin Gleede, "Vermischt, ausgetauscht und kreuzweis zugesprochen: Zur wechselhaften Geschichte der Idiome Christi in der alten Kirche," in: Bayer/Gleede, *Creator est Creatura*, 35-93, here: 37-39.

he said that "not the separated God" had died, but only God "united with humanity."

There is, finally, a third case which may well be the most interesting as well as most difficult. John had mentioned earlier in the same section that "God" and "man" are words used of universal natures whereas proper names denote individuals. This would mean expressions such as the ones Luther demanded as the test of orthodoxy ("God is dead") as well as the ones John himself used ("God was seen upon earth") were disallowed. In fact, this was a serious problem and largely responsible for centuries of doctrinal controversy following the Council of Chalcedon.[94] John of Damascus, however, pleads for a compromise here: these terms, he suggests, apply to only one nature within the divine-human person of the Incarnate, but refer to the whole hypostasis nonetheless. The terminological problem reflected an underlying doctrinal difficulty. It is undoubtedly challenging to understand how a single person partakes of both divine and human natures in such a way that both these "natures" are fully preserved, not creating a kind of divine-human halfway house, but not establishing two separate centers of personal existence either. The *communicatio idiomatum* was intended to

---

94   Johannes Zachhuber, "Christology after Chalcedon and the Transformation of the Philosophical Tradition: Reflections on a neglected topic," in Mikonja Knezevic (ed.), *The Ways of Byzantine Philosophy* (Alhambra: Sebastian Press, 2015), 103–27, here 111 ff.

facilitate language in line with these doctrinal principles. That proper names can be used interchangeably indicates the full hypostatic union in the person of Jesus Christ; that generic terms denoting natures should not be used interchangeably, on the other hand, takes into account the remaining duality of the natures even after the union.

From the thirteenth century, the scholastics accepted a shorthand formula for this complex theory. According to this rule, which appeared for the first time in Bonaventure, the communication of idioms could be applied "in the concrete but not in the abstract" form.[95] It sounds like one of those pedantic rules that have given a bad name to the thought of the schoolmen, but it served a purpose: to regulate the use of Christological language in such a way that it preserved both the union of the natures and their distinctiveness. This was evidently the form in which Luther came to know the rule.

As we have already seen, the reformer was a great advocate of this principle. In fact, he made it clear that in many ways the communication of idioms for him lay at the basis of the unique dignity of the person of the savior.[96] And yet there is perhaps no other aspect of Luther's Christology that has drawn as much criticism as his use of the communication of

---

95 Bonaventure, *In Sententiarum* I, dist. 33, a. 1, q. 3, ad 4m.

96 Cf. the various contributions to: Bayer/ Gleede (eds.), *Creator est Creatura*.

idioms. The strongest queries that have been raised about the compatibility of his Christology with the Chalcedonian tradition are based on his particular use of this form of theological language. The most famous – or notorious – case for this is his controversy about the Eucharist with the Swiss reformer Huldrych Zwingli. It ultimately boiled down to a disagreement concerning the real presence of the body of Christ in the Lord's Supper, which Luther affirmed but Zwingli denied.

2 Christology in the Controversy between Luther and Zwingli about the Eucharist

Concern about the real presence of Christ in the Eucharist was close to Luther's heart from early on.[97] Yet while it would be wrong to think that the controversy with the reformer of Zurich, Huldrych Zwingli, the Basel theologian, Johannes Oecolampadius, and others in the latter half of the 1520s was the trigger for an entirely novel departure in the reformer's thought, this debate made Luther reflect more deeply on Christology than ever before. The controversy was arguably the most consequential among early Protestants as it led to the schism, never to be healed, between the Lutheran and the

---

97   Gottfried Seebass, "Zum Hintergrund der christologischen Disputation Luthers von 1540/43," in Bayer/Gleede (eds.), *Creator est Creatura*, 125–38.

Reformed, later Calvinist, churches. Soon after these conflicts broke out, it became clear how radically different positions regarding the Eucharist were on the two sides. What is more, the conflicting interpretations of the Lord's Supper ultimately brought to light a faultline which extended far beyond this one issue affecting large parts of their theologies. Zwingli was the first to allege that Luther's affirmation of the real presence was grounded in a Christology that failed to give sufficient room to the specific dignity of Christ's humanity. Luther responded along the same lines, and the controversy soon revealed deep Christological disagreement.

Zwingli's rejection of Christ's real presence in the Lord's Supper was initially based on a non-literal interpretation of the words of institution (1 Cor 11, 24); rightly understood, the reformer from Zurich held, they established a merely symbolic relationship between the bread and the body of Christ. The host "signifies" the body, and the Eucharist therefore is more properly a memorial meal, not a sacrament.[98]

Johannes Oecolampadius was the first to add a further argument that moved the controversy into the territory of Christology; it was soon embraced by Zwingli as well. A human body, they suggested, cannot be in more than one place. After the ascension, however, Christ was "by the right hand of the Father," a passage Augustine had taught to read

---

98   Huldrych Zwingli, *De vera et falsa religione Commentarius, Corpus Reformatorum* 90:807, 11–14.

literally,[99] and this interpretation had even been in-corporated into canon law.[100] If, then, Christ's body was in heaven, it could not *also* be on earth and, by implication, not in the host either. Consequently, the real presence was impossible.

The problem was certainly not new. In the elev-enth century, Peter Lombard was already aware of opponents of the real presence who used Augus-tine's authority in the same way, but also referred to other biblical passages that became a topic of debate in the sixteenth century again, for example Mt 14, 7 ("For you always have the poor with you …; but you will not always have me") as well as John 6, 63 ("the flesh is useless").[101] Interestingly, however, the ensu-ing scholastic discussion about the real presence was largely detached from the problem of Christology.

Aquinas, but in particular William of Ockham and his students, acknowledged the difficulty of ac-counting for the presence of the body of Christ in many places, but their answers made almost no refer-

---

99   Augustine, *In Johannis Evangelium Tractatus* 30, 1,
      17.

100   *Decretum of Gratian*, part 3, *de Consecratione*, dist.
      2, c. 44, c. 1, in *Corpus Iuris Canonici I* (Graz: Akade-
      mische Druck- und Verlagsanstalt, 1959), 1330: "Cor-
      pus enim, in quo resurrexit, uno loco esse oportet."

101   Peter Lombard, *Sentences*, IV, d. 10; cf. Hartmut
      Hilgenfeld, *Mittelalterlich-traditionelle Elemente in
      Luthers Abendmahlsschriften* (Zürich: Theologischer
      Verlag, 1971), 183.

ence to the Incarnation or the communication of idioms.[102] Instead, they construed this problem largely as a special case of the spatial existence of created being. Accordingly, Ockham influentially distinguished between different senses of being in a place.[103] This was possible, he suggested, either as being whole in the whole, but only partially in the parts, or by being whole in the whole *and* also whole in each part. The former he called "circumscriptive" and the latter "definitive" presence. The definitive presence applied, for example, to the presence of the soul in the human body; we might call it "non-extended" presence. Ockham argued that the "definitive" presence could explain how Christ's human body could be in the elements of the Eucharist while also existing in the heavens considered as a physical space. The "definitive" presence, however, could at a maximum explain why the concurrent presence of the body of Christ in the heavens and on the altars did not entail a logical contradiction. The real presence as such remained a

---

102   Thomas Aquinas: *Summa Theologiae*, III, q. 76; for Ockham, e.g., *Summa Logicae*, I, 44 (121 ,4-122, 10 Boehner); *de sacramento altaris*. Cf. Hilgenfeld, *Mittelalterlich-traditionelle Elemente*, 184–94.

103   William of Ockham, *Quodlibet* 4, q. 31, in *Quodlibetal Questions*, trans. Alfred Freddoso and Francis E. Kelly (New Haven, CT: Yale University Press, 1991), 371–75. Cf. Stephen E. Lahey, "Late Medieval Eucharistic Theology," in Ian Levy et al. (eds.), *A Companion to the Eucharist in the Middle Ages* (Leiden: Brill, 2012), 499–540, here 510–11.

miracle and was usually classed with the virgin birth
and Jesus' walking through walls as examples of in-
tentional violations of the order of nature in the salvific dispensation made possible by divine omnipo-
tence.[104]

For Luther things were very different. Firstly,
Christ's real presence in the Eucharist and his in-
dissoluble, personal union in the Incarnation were
closely related; in fact, one might almost say they
were two sides of the same coin. His unwillingness
to compromise on Zwingli's doctrine of the Lord's
Supper was at least partly motivated by Luther's
sense that the rejection of the real presence undermined a proper Christology and with this the basis of the faith itself. After all, faith in Christ for
the Wittenberg reformer was based on a true encounter with the savior, and such an encounter with
Christ was the gateway to any knowledge of God.
But Christ, for Luther, was conceivable only in his
divine-human unity. At the Marburg Colloquy, the
1529 attempt at peace-making involving Luther,
Zwingli, Melanchthon, Oecolampadius and others,
Luther summed up his view by saying that he "did
not know or worship any God except him who was
made man; nor did he want to have another God besides him. And besides him there was no other God
who could save us."[105] Christ was the foundation

---

104   Cf. Ockham, *de sacr. alt.* 6; cf. Hilgenfeld, *Mittelal-
       terlich-traditionelle Elemente*, 194.

105   LW 38, 46.

of the Christian faith precisely because God had committed in him to a firm and permanent union with humanity. Before Luther even entered into any technicalities, he was emphatic that denying the real presence was tantamount to severing the hypostatic union and thus took away the ground for the hope of salvation:

> If you could show me one place where God is and not the man, then the person is already divided and I could at once say truthfully, "Here is God who is not man and has never become man." But no God like that for me! For it would follow from this that space and place had separated the two natures from one another and thus had divided the person, even though death and all the devils had been unable to separate and tear them apart.[106]

This insistence on a straight link between real presence and Christology, secondly, brought the communication of idioms to the fore of Luther's argument. When in the course of the controversy, his opponents accused Luther of a failure properly to distinguish the two natures in Christ, the Wittenberg reformer retorted that he kept divinity and humanity distinct, but at the same time believed in the unity of the person and therefore confessed that "God is man and man is God."[107] In other words, he appealed to the *communicatio idiomatum*. It was this hermeneuti-

---

106   LW 37, 218.

107   LW 37, 212.

cal principle which Luther felt would vindicate his stance. As he was to find out, however, things were rather more ambivalent than he seemed to think.

Initially, Luther's wording was carefully calibrated to the rules generally accepted for the communication of idioms:

> You must say that the person (pointing to Christ) suffers, and dies. But this person is truly God, and therefore it is correct to say: the Son of God suffers. Although, so to speak, the one part (namely, the divinity) does not suffer, nevertheless the person, who is God, suffers in the other part (namely, in the humanity).[108]

Put in this way, however, the rule did not explain the real presence, as Christ's human nature does not partake of divine properties and would therefore appear unable to be in two places at the same time. Luther therefore took a fateful further step in his argument. The "right hand of the Father," he suggested, must be everywhere, like the divinity itself. If therefore Christ was at the right hand of the Father, he must be everywhere too, for the simple reason that to suggest otherwise would be to split up the unity of his divine-human person:

> Here you must take your stand and say that wherever Christ is according to his divinity, he is there as a natural, divine person and he is also naturally and personally there ... But if he is pres-

---

108   LW 37, 210.

> ent naturally and personally wherever he is, then
> he must be man there, too, since he is not two
> separate persons but a single person. Wherever
> this person is, it is the single, indivisible person,
> and if you can say, "Here is God," then you must
> also say, Christ the man is present too.[109]

This may have seemed to Luther a straightforward
way of insisting on the personal unity of Christ to
explain the necessity of the real presence. Yet the
Christological consequences were potentially far-
reaching. By arguing that Christ is everywhere "even
according to his humanity," Luther apparently over-
stepped the limits of the classical communication of
idioms as he himself had earlier spelled them out:
predicates can be mutually applied *in concreto* but
not *in abstracto*. Behind this rule, however, as we have
seen, stood the dual boundary drawn by the Council
of Chalcedon according to which the two natures are
united "without confusion, without change, without
division, without separation." By calling Christ's human nature present "wherever Christ is according
to his divinity," Luther seems to have pandered to a
view of Jesus Christ in which the lasting distinction
of the natures is given up in the interest of a one-sided insistence on their personal unity. We shall have
to come back to this.

   In the scholarly literature, much has been made of
a third plank in Luther's argument. For in support of
his controversial claims, the reformer went on to em-

---

109   LW 37, 218.

ploy more technical language, clearly related to the
earlier scholastic discussion. He offered a distinction
between three ways something can be in a place: "lo-
cally or circumscriptively, definitively, repletively."[110]
The first was physical presence of an object in space;
the second, a presence within a limited space but in
a non-physical manner. The third manner belongs
to the Godhead, which is everywhere whole but not
contained by any local circumscription. Christ, Luther argued, partook of all three types, notably after
the ascension in the third:

> Since he is a man who is supernaturally one person
> with God, and apart from this man there is no
> God, it must follow that according to the third
> supernatural mode, he is and can be wherever God
> is and that everything is full of Christ through
> and through, even according to his humanity.[111]

This is the fateful notion of the ubiquity of Christ's
human nature after the resurrection, a view not only
sharply repudiated by Zwingli and later by Calvin,
but deeply controversial and divisive even within
the Lutheran camp itself. It has been called the "new
dogma" of Lutheranism (Heinrich Bullinger[112]), and

---

110   LW 37, 215.

111   LW 37, 218.

112   Cf. Theodor Mahlmann, *Das neue Dogma der
       lutherischen Christologie: Problem und Geschichte seiner
       Begründung* (Gütersloh: Gütersloher Verlagshaus,
       1969), 9.

this was not meant as a compliment. Others have slated him for calling in "the aid of Occam's scholasticism" (Harnack[113]) in order to score points against his Protestant opponents.

It is possible, however, to overstate Luther's dependence on Ockham and the Ockhamists in his Eucharistic theology. He did not share Ockham's definition of "definitive presence," and for his own argument the "repletive presence" was more important anyway. The latter is altogether absent from Ockham, and where it occurs in later thinkers this is not to explain real presence but as a mode of *divine* presence in the world.[114] This points to the more important difference. As we have seen, the possibility of the real presence, for Aquinas, Ockham, and all those after him was a physical and ultimately a metaphysical problem; for Luther, however, it was ultimately a corollary of the Incarnation, an application of the *communicatio idiomatum*, however idiosyncratic. While there was ultimately no theory that could explain why this body was present in the host and not elsewhere – and Luther was entirely willing to take this simply on the authority of the biblical word of promise – the theoretical vehicle he is will-

---

113   Adolf von Harnack, *History of Dogma*, trans. Neil Buchanan, vol. 7 (London: Williams & Norgate, 1899), 262.

114   Gabriel Biel, coll. I, d. 37, q. una; Hilgenfeld, *Mittelalterlich-traditionelle Elemente*, 200–203.

ing to use derives from his long-held view[115] that the
body of Christ partook of a particular glory as a result of its union with the divine.

Perhaps it is also going too far to attribute to Luther a *theory* of the ubiquity of Christ's human nature; ultimately, this claim for him was never more
than a prop to sustain a belief he held for rather
different reasons. The fact, however, remains that
he was seemingly unconcerned to vitiate against
the principle of the communication of idioms in its
traditional guise. Does this indicate, as some have
suspected, that his underlying Christology is monophysite? Before such a conclusion is drawn, however,
some mitigating reflections can be helpful. First of
all, it appears that the history of Christian thought
up to Luther, while usually affirming the real presence in the Eucharist, has hardly been able to explain it in a more satisfactory way. Luther's hunch
to connect it with the hypostatic union of the Incarnate is certainly closer to Patristic witnesses than
the medieval speculations about the spatial presence
of Christ's body. While it is arguably impossible
to know what precisely the Church Fathers meant
when they spoke of the "life-giving flesh" of the glo-
rified savior as present in the Eucharist, it would
seem plausible to assume that they implicitly considered Christ's humanity to share the ubiquity of the

---

115   Cf. WA 6, 510,7; Hilgenfeld, *Mittelalterlich-traditionelle Elemente*, 205.

Godhead after the ascension.[116] Luther's theological intuition in recovering the connection between real presence and the Incarnation is surely that of a "reformer" in the literal sense even if it were the case that his theoretical foundation was flawed.

One may, however, possibly go a step further and query how inviolable the scholastic version of the *communicatio idiomatum* is. We have seen that John of Damascus was aware that the potentially most significant cases, such as "God died on the cross," let alone the famous *theotokos*, were at best only accounted for as borderline legitimate. For it could easily be argued that "God" was in fact a word signifying "nature," not "person." A rigid application of the scholastic rule might therefore reach a solution very similar to that proposed by Nestorius according to which terms denoting the divine nature cannot be said of humanity, and *vice versa*; that, however, terms specifically denoting the person of the Incarnate can be applied to both his divine and human aspects.[117] Mary, consequently, would be neither *theotokos*, nor *anthropotokos*, but *christotokos*. Cyril's anathemas

---

116   For Cyril of Alexandria, see Henry Chadwick, "Christology and Eucharist in the Nestorian Controversy," *Journal of Theological Studies* n.s. 11 (1951): 145–64, here 153–57. Note that the Formula of Concord lists a considerable number of Patristic statements in support of the Lutheran position: http://bookofconcord.org/testimonies.php.

117   Gleede, *Creator est Creatura*, 59.

were directed against this very solution, and the
Council of Ephesus followed him in this decision.[118]

The point is not, of course, to accuse the medieval
advocates of the *communicatio idiomatum* of Nestori-
anism, but to point out that the distinction of *abstract*
natures and the *concrete* person on which it relies is
itself not without its problems. What is the person
if not the concrete realization of a nature? From its
origins, Chalcedon has been accused of severing this
vital link between individual (hypostasis or person)
and nature, thereby affirming a savior who is neither
properly divine nor properly human.[119]

Luther, it is increasingly becoming clear, combined
a commitment to traditional Christology with a
willingness to push against its limits in the interest
of the personal unity of divine and human in the savior without which, he was convinced, there could be
no salvation. At the same time, however, there may
be reasons also to query the legitimacy of these very
limits and boundaries not in a neo-Protestant, liberal interest of abolishing dogma – this clearly was
not what Luther aimed at – but rather by recogniz-
ing their tensional relationship already in the early
Church with the need to express the underlying
kerygma of the crucified God.

---

118   ACO I, 1, 1, 41, 1–4.

119   Zachhuber, "Christology after Chalcedon,"
        113–15.

3 Contours of a Systematic Christology: The Late Christological Disputations

Throughout much of his life, Luther's evident concern for Christological problems was not matched by a willingness to engage in detail with the technicalities of this doctrine as they had developed over at least one thousand years. Yet from 1533 academic disputations resumed at the University of Wittenberg, and several of those gave Luther the opportunity to express himself more clearly about this matter. While it would be wrong to consider these texts as Luther's most authentic statements on Christology, they are invaluable for any attempt to inscribe his thought into previous doctrinal developments and to gauge the extent to which his Christology is compatible with earlier traditions.

Importantly, the overall tendency of Luther's Christological arguments in these disputations conforms with his occasional references as well as the implications gathered from his pronouncements on other theological topics throughout his career. Luther's main concern is with the personal union of divine and human in Jesus Christ. He is uncompromising in his rejection of any attempts to mitigate or tone down the radical and paradoxical consequences this union has. In Jesus, we encounter both God and man; we encounter the eternal, impassible God suffering and mortal. And we encounter the man Jesus who can equally be called the creator of the world.

Luther is scathing in his rejection of the Ockhamists and their theory of suppositional union.[120]
William of Ockham had been concerned that the
traditional hypostatic union seemed to imply that, in
the assumption, Christ's human nature was merged
with the divine person of the Word. On the one
hand, this could jettison the lasting independence of
Christ's humanity; on the other, it was unclear how
a "personal union" was even possible given the radical
distinction between divine and human natures. Ockham therefore introduced the notion of a "supposite,"
an ontological foundation of concrete existence, and
stipulated a union of divine and human natures at
that level rather than the personal level. In the incarnation, consequently, the divinity provides such a
"suppositional," existential basis for Christ's humanity, but does not assume it into its own personality.[121]

Ockhamist Christology has often been seen as a
seeking a quasi-Nestorian corrective to the Christologies of the high scholastic period by emphasizing more strongly the reality of Christ's humanity.[122]
Luther, however, fastened on their rejection of the

---

120   WA 39/II, 95, 32–36.

121   Reinhard Schwarz, "Gott und Mensch: Zur Lehre
      von der Person Christi bei den Ockhamisten und bei
      Luther," *Zeitschrift für Theologie und Kirche* 63 (1966):
      289–351, here 293–301.

122   Heiko A. Oberman, *Harvest of Medieval Theology:
      Gabriel Biel and Late Medieval Nominalism* (Cam-
      bridge, MA: Harvard University Press, 1963), 258.

personal union and consequently accused the Ockhamists of denying Christ's true humanity.[123] Yet even more than the details of their theory, it was its philosophical cast that worried Luther. Where scripture teaches us to speak of the Word becoming flesh (John 1, 14), and the councils developed this into the language of two natures in one person, the rigor of their logical and grammatical theories forced the Ockhamists, in Luther's view, to develop doctrines that were as artificial as they were remote from the foundations of the Christian faith. This animus finds expression in categorical statements about the irreconcilability of theology and philosophy.[124]

Yet it would be facile to overlook Luther's dependence on this same tradition within which, after all, he had been raised.[125] First, there is his concern with the language of Christology. In the disputation about Christ's divinity and humanity he includes several theses about the need to acknowledge that in Christology, theologians speak a "new language" which is different from the language of philosophy (Th. 20–24).[126] This demand might seem to jar with his concurrent criticism of the scholastics' tendency

---

123   WA 39/II, 95, 34–36; cf. Schwarz, "Gott und Mensch," 301–302.

124   Cf. WA 39/II, 3, 3.7.

125   Theodor Dieter, "Luther as a Late Medieval Theologian," in *The Oxford Handbook of Martin Luther's Theology*, 31–48, here 34–35.

126   WA 39/II, 94, 17–25.

to take refuge in equivocation in order to explain the mystery of the Incarnation.[127] Yet Luther's distinction between old and new language is driven not by the ontological chasm between infinite God and finite creation, but by the logic of the history of salvation. Calling Christ a creature is wrong and indeed heretical (Arian) according to the "old" language because it detaches him from God (Th. 27–28).[128] The same statement, however, is correct and significant in the "new" language because it denotes the outcome of God's salvific act: the theologian has to affirm that in Christ creator and creature have become reconciled (Th. 22).[129]

Most significant was, once again, Luther's reference of the communication of idioms, which he adapted from his sometime Ockhamist teachers.[130] We must here consider his disputation *On the Divinity and the Humanity of Christ* (1540). Right after the reformer's affirmation of the *fides catholica* that there is "one Lord Christ, truly God and man" (Th. 1), he claims that the communication of idioms "follows" from this fundamental truth (Th. 2).[131] He goes on to spell out the specifics of the doctrine: it is right

---

127   E.g. WA 39/II, 10, 25–32 C; 17, 2–7 A.

128   WA 39/II, 94, 31–33.

129   WA 39/II, 94, 21.

130   For the views of the Ockhamists cf. Schwarz, "Gott und Mensch," 313–18.

131   WA 39/II, 93, 2–4.

to say, "This man created the world" and, "This God suffered, died, was buried etc." (Th. 4).[132] But we cannot exchange the idioms of the abstract natures, only of the concrete person (Th. 5).[133] Luther therefore polemicized against Caspar von Schwenckfeld, who taught that Christ's humanity was spiritualized in and through the Incarnation: a case of an extreme communication of idioms between the two natures. Luther's affirmation of Chalcedonian orthodoxy in that context was no formality: he fully held that the paradox of the Incarnation was possible only if both notions – the distinction of divine and human *and* their union – were asserted with equal firmness.

At the same time, however, we find Luther once again transgressing the limits of the traditional communication of idioms. He did so in his dispute with Zwingli by gesturing at the ubiquity of Christ's human nature on the basis of the communication of idioms, and he does so again in his late disputations:

> God gives us figures of speech according to which Christ is God and man in one person. There are not two persons, but two natures united in one person in such a way that what applies to human nature, can be said to apply to the divine nature, and *vice versa* (*Dedit Deus nobis formulas loquendi, quod Christus sit Deus et homo in una persona, et non sunt duae personae, sed duae naturae unitae sunt*

---

132   WA 39/II, 93, 8.

133   WA 39/II, 93, 10.

> *in una persona sic, ut, quod ab humana natura fit,*
> *dicatur etiam fieri a divina, et e contra.).*[134]

This is not a slip of his pen. For Luther, the communication of idioms between the two natures
ultimately confirms the reality of the union. The
distinction between nature and person, while valid
and important up to a point, for him is also problematical because it can appear as a caveat, a qualification of the personal union. While many of his
predecessors accepted the theopaschite formula only
by adding immediately "according to his humanity,"
Luther's viewpoint is the reverse: "God himself has
truly suffered" for him is indubitably, albeit paradoxically, true, and the qualification "according to the humanity which he assumed," while formally correct, is
ultimately of secondary importance.[135]

If Luther thus relativized the strict dichotomy of
nature and person in Christological theory in the interest of a strong emphasis on the personal union,
we find a countervailing tendency in his references
to the character of the union. Neo-Chalcedonian
orthodoxy had decreed that the one person of the
God-man was the divine hypostasis within which
the human nature subsisted (*enhypostaton*) without
a hypostasis of its own (*anhypostaton*). Once again,
we find Luther affirming this tenet without qualification: "Christ is man, that is a divine person taking

---

134   WA 98, 14–17.

135   Cf. Schwarz, "Gott und Mensch," 312.

on human nature" (Arg. 27).[136] At the same time, however, he is using language that sounds very different, emphasizing much more a symmetrical relationship between God and man in the one person: "that person is God and man" (*illa persona est deus et homo*: Arg. 2);[137] or even more provocatively, "humanity and divinity constitute one person in Christ" (*humanitas et divinitas in Christo constituunt unam personam*: Arg. 1).[138] Luther, who had accused the Ockhamists of being Eutychians, evidently felt it important to give due weight to the human element in Christ's single person, but in doing so he pushed again against the limits of established (Neo-)Chalcedonian orthodoxy.[139]

4 Conclusion

It is on account of cases like this that Luther's critical readers have argued that he deviated from the accepted norms of the Catholic tradition. In this interpretation, his willingness to push the limits of the communication of idioms indicates something more serious: that in his insistence on the indivis-

---

136 WA 39/II, 117, 35–36 B.

137 WA 39/II, 101, 10 B.

138 WA 39/II, 100, 18 B.

139 Axel Schmidt, *Die Christologie in Martin Luthers späten Disputationen* (St. Ottilien: EOS Verlag, 1990), 246–47.

ible unity of divine and human in Jesus Christ, Luther neglected the need to distinguish between what was divine and what was human in the savior. In this way, he would have approached the position of those opponents of the Council of Chalcedon which the Catholic Church has called monophysites, in other words those who maintain only one single nature in the person of Christ.

Yet if Luther seems to pander to the right of Chalcedonian orthodoxy, there is also evidence that he tended to its left. This evidence, as we have seen, takes the form of references in Luther's works to the person of Christ as a divine-human compound. Such language was suspect as placing too much emphasis on the equality of divine and human in Christ; in its place, the Church preferred the doctrine that the savior's single hypostasis was, in fact, his divine personality into which his humanity was merely inserted.

There is, then, a tension at the heart of Luther's Christology: on the one hand, he willingly and explicitly followed the path trodden by Catholic Christianity since the Patristic period, for which the communication of idioms was aligned with the distinction between the *duality* of natures and the *singularity* of the person, and the one person of Christ was the hypostasis of the Logos. On the other hand, he pushed against the limits drawn in this process or even transgressed them. Both liberal and more conservative readers have concluded from this observation that ultimately Luther's Christology cannot be reconciled with received orthodoxy, whatever his own intentions may have been.[140] More plausible, however, is another interpretation. Luther situated his Christology within the Chalcedonian tradition, but his attitude toward this tradition was more flexible because he perceived doctrinal decisions as ultimately deriving from scripture and therefore in need of justification in light of the biblical testimony.[141] Luther had no reason to think that Chalcedon had falsified the Bible's witness to Jesus Christ, but it did have the potential to curtail it, as the formally orthodox Christologies of the "scholastics" showed. Its teaching therefore had to be adapted to the apparent truths revealed in scripture. For Luther these were, as has been seen throughout this article, the reality of human and divine in Christ, their personal unity, and the resulting communication of idioms. Only on this basis, he knew, was salvation possible, and any Christology worth its salt had fully to account for these facts.

At the outset of this lecture I asked how it could have been possible that Luther's single-minded focus on Jesus Christ as the one center of the Chris-

---

140   Holl, "Was verstand Luther unter Religion?" in Holl, *Gesammelte Aufsätze zur Kirchengeschichte*, vol. 1, 6th ed. (Tübingen: Mohr Siebeck, 1932), 71; Yves Congar, "Regards et réflexions sur la christologie de Luther."

141   Cf. LW 41, 119.

tian faith and the exclusive cause of human salvation could be controversial or even lead to the break-up of ecclesial unity. It now becomes perhaps a little clearer how this was possible, as his attempt to explicate the Christological basis of his Christocentrism led the reformer to concepts that were more than occasionally violating the rules drawn by the earlier doctrinal tradition of the Catholic Church. They were also, it should be noted, tensional amongst themselves. Does it then follow that Luther was either seriously in error or that he inaugurated the departure of modern Christianity from its doctrinal heritage? I think a different answer is possible if we are willing to accept that there is an underlying tension in any attempt to tie together Christianity's focus on the uniquely central place of the person of Jesus Christ as humanity's savior with a doctrinal formula seeking to capture the nature of this individual. Both are arguably necessary, but as much as a Christocentric emphasis pushes against the limits of any formulaic Christology, attempts to define such a formula create difficulties in accounting for the fullness of the Christian experience as related to Jesus Christ.

In what follows, I shall explore this hypothesis in two directions. I shall firstly show how the consolidation of dogmatic Christology, almost exactly one thousand years prior to the Reformation, was in itself a tensional and problematic process whose gain in conceptual clarity was paid for in a loss of a full sense of Christocentric faith. Subsequently, I shall make the argument in a more systematic form by showing how Christology as a theory about a uniquely significant individual constantly and necessarily pushes against the limits posed by metaphysical theology.

4 Tensions at the Origins of
Christology

In the fifth century, the entire Eastern Church was
gripped by a fierce controversy about the right way
to speak and teach about the person of Jesus Christ.
Almost exactly one thousand years before Luther's
birth, in 482, the Roman Emperor Zeno made one
more, rather desperate attempt to bring the warring
factions together by issuing an edict, called the *Heno-
tikon*.[142] Yet in the end, this as well as other attempts
at reconciliation failed. We today are often inclined
the see the Reformation of the sixteenth century as
the major schismatic epoch in the Church's history;
those who know their history are also aware that the
Eastern and Western Churches parted ways in the
eleventh century. Only few understand, however,
how massive and deeply traumatic the schism was
that ensued from the Christological controversies in
the fifth century. Part of the reason for this negli-
gence is that the arena of this conflict was overrun,
only some centuries later, by the Arab invasion and
its population eventually became majority Muslim.
Recent news has, however, reminded us, albeit for
entirely tragic reasons, of the continuing existence
of these Eastern Churches that were separated from
the Byzantine and the Roman churches during this
period, never to be reconciled with them again.

142   Grillmeier, *Jesus der Christus im Glauben der Kirche*, II/1, 285–90.

At the time, this was by no means a marginal event. Rather, the provinces that broke away from the Byzantine Church were some of the oldest and most thoroughly Christian parts of the Eastern world including Egypt, parts of Palestine, Syria, Armenia, Ethiopia, and others. In other words, the fallout was in no way less cataclysmic than the schism of the sixteenth century. Why did it happen? At the danger of simplifying a little, this question can be answered in one word: Chalcedon. The Council of 451 was extremely unpopular in the Christian East.[143] There were inevitably various reasons for this unpopularity, not all of them theological, but the theological and doctrinal objections were certainly strong. The Christological formula of the Council, mandating the language of two natures, divine and human in the person of Jesus Christ, was seen by many as effectively giving up on the personal, individual union in the savior which, they believed, was key for salvation. The most important witness cited by the critics of the Council was Cyril of Alexandria, probably the greatest Christological thinker of the Greek Church. Cyril died in 444, so was not present at the Council whose decisions were instead inspired by the Pope Leo the Great. While Chalcedon made nods in the direction of Cyril's theology, the majority of his fol-

---

143 Grillmeier, *Jesus der Christus im Glauben der Kirche*, II/1, 107–375.

lowers felt that it was, in fact, a betrayal of his theological insight.[144]

The purpose of this chapter is not, of course, to give an exhaustive overview of the developments of this period. Nor do I intend to argue that Patristic Christologies were hopelessly muddled and contradictory. Instead, I hope to illuminate Luther's tensional relationship with the tradition of Chalcedonian Christology by setting it into this historical context. Throughout this lecture I have sought to suggest that Luther's thought can profitably be set side by side with that of the Church Fathers. This claim can be extended by observing that Luther's Christocentrism is also matched by that of the early church. Doctrinal developments in the first centuries were largely driven by a series of attempts to find agreement on conceptualizations of this tenet or, differently put, on a theological language capable of expressing this deeply held tenet of the Christian faith. If it is thus difficult to comprehend why Luther's attempt radically to put Jesus Christ at the center of Christian faith and practice could ever have been led to controversy and division, the same riddle is posed by the development of Christology in the Patristic period as well.

144   W. H. C. Frend, *The Rise of the Monophysite Movement: Chapters in the History of the Church in the Fifth and Sixth Centuries* (Cambridge: CUP, 1972); Joseph Lebon, "La christologie du monophysisme syrien," in Grillmeier/Bacht, *Das Konzil von Chalkedon*, 1, 425–580.

There is, admittedly, a strong tradition in both Catholic and Protestant theologies that considers doctrinal development in a progressive paradigm. On this reading, doctrinal conflict is due to insufficient conceptual clarification; later articulations of the same doctrine are therefore inherently superior in that they resolve problems that earlier representatives of orthodoxy had failed to clarify. Yet while it is perhaps impossible not to admire the intellectual creativity invested into increasingly elaborate philosophical and theological interpretations of the Christian faith over the centuries, there is little evidence that the ensuing complex syntheses ever resolved genuine disagreements.

In his classical history of Christology, the nineteenth-century German theologian Isaak August Dorner argued for a different approach and opined that the Christologies of the pre-Chalcedonian period, while inevitably less sophisticated, were often more faithful to the *Christusbild* (image of Christ) of the Bible than were later, more conceptually refined accounts.[145] As we shall see, it is arguable that, as tensional Christologies gave way to condemnations and the establishment of separate churches from the fifth century, conceptual clarity was paid for with the exclusion of theologically vital perspectives. In this sense, we might at least be open to the possibility

---

145   Isaak August Dorner, *Entwicklungsgeschichte der Lehre von der Person Christi* (Stuttgart: Liesching, 1845), vol. 1, xxvii–xxviii.

that the cracks visible in Luther's Christology indicate an attempt to reach back to an early period of doctrinal development in the interest of recovering a base for his radical vision of *solus Christus* which later Christologies could no longer sustain.

1 The Council of Chalcedon and Its Opponents

To the eyes of a Western Christian, rejection of the Council of Chalcedon must seem as implausible as the Arian opposition to Nicaea. Balancing an affirmation of the full humanity and divinity of the savior with a confession to their union in his single hypostasis or person, the Council appears to have found a formula that gives due weight to all aspects of the Christological problem. Who would oppose such a formula except those who preferred to neglect either Christ's full humanity or his single personality? In this sense, non-Chalcedonians have for centuries been labeled as "monophysites" and "Nestorians," heresies committing those two complementary errors.

Historical scholarship – as well as ecumenical dialogue with non-Chalcedonian churches – has succeeded over the past century in radically changing this perception.[146] The Coptic, Syriac and other

---

146   The single most influential study in this regard has been Joseph Lebon, *Le monophysisme sévérien: étude historique, littéraire et théologique sur la resistance mono-*

ecclesiastical communions following the lead of bishops such as Severus of Antioch were not "monophysite" opponents of Christ's humanity, but understood themselves as faithful followers of Cyril of Alexandria and with him preferred the phrase "one nature" (μία φύσις) when speaking of the Incarnate. In doing so, their primary theological concern was the full affirmation of the personal, hypostatic union of divine and human in the savior, not a neglect of his humanity. Chalcedon, which pointedly did not receive Cyril's Twelve Anathemas against Nestorius while insisting on the perseverance of two natures after the union, did not seem to honor this commitment.

This was by no means a mere disagreement about formulae. Insisting on a single nature in the Incarnate, the opponents of Chalcedon felt they were defending the concrete character of natures and their direct relationship with individual persons. A famous battle-cry consequently demanded that there could be "no physis without hypostasis."[147] Two natures in the Incarnate would therefore inevitably mean two persons – in effect a denial of the hypostatic union. The Chalcedonians of course rejected this inference – and sincerely so; but their search for an alternative

---

physite sur la concile de Chalcédoine (Leuven: Linthout, 1909).

147 References for this motto in Uwe Lang, *John Philoponus and the Controversies over Chalcedon in the Sixth Century* (Leuven: Peeters, 2001), 63.

took centuries, and their ultimate solution treated the "natures" in such an abstract manner that it could easily appear that the single hypostasis or person was as detached from one as it was from the other.[148]

This detachment of abstract natures from the concrete person was, as we have seen, precisely the concern underlying Luther's push against the limits of the language of the communication of idioms. If it is arguable on those grounds that he vitiated against the boundaries set by the language of Chalcedon, it is perhaps worth mentioning that the Scythian monks, that same group which successfully propagated the use of the theopaschite formula in the sixth century, proposed as well the conditional use of the *mia physis* formula as another way of securing the appropriate integration of Cyril's theological heritage in the Byzantine Church.[149] In this they were obviously – and probably rightly – unsuccessful, but the mere attempt shows how closely the emphasis on God's paradoxical suffering in the flesh, the tradition of Cyril's anti-Nestorian Christology and the miaphysite opposition to Chalcedon, were historically connected.

There is yet another side to this development, however, that has to be taken into consideration. The Council of Chalcedon also cemented the separation

---

148   Zachhuber, "Christology after Chalcedon," 124–26.

149   Grillmeier, *Jesus der Christus im Glauben der Kirche*, II/2, 346-47.

of the Byzantine Church – and with it the Western Church – from the so-called Nestorian Church of the East which remained predominant in today's Iraq, Persia and in areas further East. In this way, the Antiochene theological tradition, an important resource for the careful attention to the human reality of the Incarnate, was increasingly lost. This tendency only increased in the sixth century when attempts by the Emperor Justinian to win back the Cyrillian, miaphysite churches included wide-ranging condemnations of Antiochene theologians, including Theodore of Mopsuestia and Theodoret of Cyrrhus.

2 Luther and Cyril of Alexandria

How can Luther be inscribed into this complex situation, and how can this help deal with the ambiguities detected in his Christology? An obvious starting point is to note the parallels between his position and that of Cyril of Alexandria. These similarities have often been observed; in fact, they extend far beyond Christology in the technical sense. They appear particularly distinctly if Cyril's theology is seen as arising from a close study of the Gospel of John with a twin focus on Eucharistic doctrine as well as the Trinity. Such an interpretation of the Alexandrian theologian has been proposed by Henry Chadwick, who opined that Eucharistic theology was the "nerve centre" of Cyril's thought,[150] and while subsequent scholarship has not always entirely agreed with the priority he gave to sacramental theology,[151] the connections he observed remain highly pertinent.

Long before Cyril became engaged in the Nestorian controversy, the sacramental emphasis of his theology was evident. In his *Commentary on the Gospel of John*, written at some point between 425 and 428,[152] Cyril went out of his way to put his Christology into the context of a theory of salvation centered on a particular understanding of the Eucharist. In the Eucharist, Cyril insists, we eat Christ's divine body, and it is by means of this ritual that we obtain redemption from death and corruption.[153] In Christ, divine and human natures had to become indivisibly one in order for salvation in this sense to

---

150   Chadwick, "Christology and Eucharist in the Nestorian Controversy," 152–56.

151   Daniel A. Keating, *The Appropriation of Divine Life in Cyril of Alexandria* (Oxford: Oxford University Press, 2004), 96.

152   Cyril of Alexandria, *Commentary on John*, trans. David R. Maxwell, ed. Joel C. Elowsky (Downers Grove, IL: Intervarsity, 2015), xvi–xvii. On dating Cyril's early writings see G. Jouassard, "L'activité littéraire de Saint Cyrille d'Alexandrie jusqu'à 428," in *Mélanges E. Podechard* (Lyon: Facultés catholiques, 1945), 159–74.

153   Cyril of Alexandria, *In Iohannem* 6, 35 (PG 73, 520 D).

be possible.[154] In other words, only a strongly unitive Christology that is properly guarded against the
possibility that Christ somehow remained a duality
of persons after the union, enabled a doctrine of the
Eucharist capable of explaining how the transformation of Christ's humanity would be passed on to the
individual believer. If there was room for doubt regarding the divine-human union in the savior, Cyril
would charge, it was altogether unclear why the Eucharist was anything other than "cannibalism" (ἀν-
θρωποφαγία) that would do nothing to redeem us
from the fate brought about us by the Fall.[155]

A realist interpretation of the words of institution, therefore, was essential. Christ said, "this is
my body," and not, Cyril observes in his exegesis of
Matthew 26, 27, "what you see is a figure" (τύπον
εἶναι τὰ φαινόμενα) because only the real presence of Christ's body and blood at the Lord's Supper
would guarantee that we receive Christ's "lifegiving
and sanctifying power," which ultimately overcomes
human mortality and leads to our resurrection and
eternal life.[156] The later anti-Nestorian anathemas
elucidate the link of this view with Christology
when they condemn anyone denying that "the flesh
gives life because it is that of the Word who gives

---

154   Cyril, *In Iohannem* 6, 64 (PG 73, 604 B-D).

155   Cyril, *c. Nestorium* IV, 4, 5 (ACO I, 1, 6, 84, 35-
37).

156   Cyril, *In Matthaeum* 26, 27 (PG 72, 452 D).

life to all" (eleventh anathema).[157] Cyril's strong sacramental realism and his equally strong emphasis on the union of divine and human in the Incarnate are really only two sides of the same coin.

It is inevitably fascinating to consider Luther's thought in light of this evident parallel; in fact, Luther himself could not resist the comparison and late in his life spoke of Zwingli as another Nestorius who had to be resisted as much as the Council of Ephesus anathematized the historical Patriarch of Constantinople.[158] Luther's view of Christ, as we have seen throughout this lecture, drew on Johannine language and consequently emphasized the closeness of the union of divinity and humanity. And as for Cyril before him, the real presence in the Eucharist seemed to Luther essential to underwrite such a Christology. Both men also shared a strongly soteriological approach to Christology, which the doctrine of the Eucharist, one might say, only serves to highlight. Salvation, they both taught, was impossible unless Christians could be sure that in Jesus Christ they encountered both God and man at the same time.

This impression is further confirmed by observing how both theologians have also been accused of being at least equivocal on divine passibility.[159] In fact,

---

157   ACO I, 1,1, 41, 28–42, 2.

158   WA 50, 591,9–16 (= LW 41, 105).

159   For Luther cf. Weinandy, *Does God Change?*, 105.
        For Cyril cf. *ep. ad Succensum* II, 4 (ACO I, 1, 6, 161,
        6–13).

this was one of the main objections the Antiochenes brought against Cyril's position, due to his radical willingness to employ paradoxical language when speaking of God's presence in the flesh. And while Nestorius was no doubt wrong to allege that Cyril believed that Christ's humanity was of the same nature as his divinity,[160] he was evidently irked by the Alexandrian's unwillingness to admit any of the statements the Antiochenes proposed to guarantee divine impassibility in the Incarnation.[161]

These parallels extend to some rather detailed points of convergence, as when both use the biblical evidence of the involvement of Christ's body in his healing ministry as proof that Scripture seeks to guard us against separating Christ's human from his divine activities. Cyril argues that Christ touched Peter's mother-in-law even though he could have healed her as God simply by exercising his will;[162] in his *Commentary on John* he makes a similar observation to explain why Jesus uses his hand to raise Jairus's daughter.[163] Luther advanced a similar line of argument in his writing against Zwingli in the interest of supporting his own, unitive Christology:

---

160   Nestorius, *Liber Heraclides*, 37; cf. Chadwick, "Christology and Eucharist in the Nestorian Controversy," 157.

161   Cf. the sequence of Nestorius's second and Cyril's third letters.

162   Cyril, *In Lucam* 4, 38 (PG 72, 552 B; 549 D).

163   Cyril, *In Iohannem* 6, 54 (PG 78, 577 C).

> For the act of touching was not useless when
> the woman who suffered from a hemorrhage
> touched the hem of Christ's garment [Matt. 9:20
> f.]. Otherwise we would also have to say that she
> did not touch Christ's hem because touching is
> of no avail.[164]

It is not implausible that Luther knew some of Cyril's writings; the Alexandrian's works were available to him in Wittenberg in a Latin translation, and while we do not seem to have any direct evidence that he read them – by contrast, we do know that Melanchthon made use of Cyril's commentary on John in his own *Annotationes in Johannem* (1523) – there are considerable indications to suggest that Luther may have been an avid reader of the Greek Fathers.[165] He certainly alluded to Cyril and to his theological positions on various occasions throughout his career, notably at the Marburg Colloquy where he claimed Cyril's support for his own cause against Zwingli.[166]

There is, then, but little doubt that Luther's and Cyril's Christologies share many features. Both approach the doctrine of the person of Christ from the point of view of the doctrine of salvation. Both

---

164   WA 26, 355, 22-26; LW 37, 238-39.

165   Carl Beckwith, "Martin Luther's Christological Sources in the Church Fathers," *Oxford Research Encyclopedia of Religion*, online at: http://religion.oxfordre.com/view/10.1093/acrefore/9780199340378.001.0001/acrefore-9780199340378-e-372: 5–7.

166   WA 26, 362, 21; LW 37, 242.

consequently emphasize the need to affirm the paradoxical unity of divine and human in the redeemer without which, they both insist, there is no salvation. Both also use freely and extensively the language of divine suffering in the Incarnate, the so-called theopaschite formula. For Cyril, the willingness to push this kind of language to the limits of paradox is a necessary condition of orthodoxy, and he was willing to break the unity of the church over this doctrinal affirmation.

The similarities extend further. We have seen how closely Luther's provocative emphasis on the insoluble personal unity of Jesus Christ is bound up with his insistence on his real presence in the Eucharist. It is therefore intriguing to note that for Cyril too Eucharistic theology was a major factor influencing the uncompromising nature of his Christological stance. Ultimately, both theologians found the basis of their understanding of the person of Christ in a theological reading of the Gospel of John; this, I believe, is their deepest and most profound commonality.

I have pointed out that many of Cyril's followers rejected the decisions of the Council of Chalcedon. It would, nevertheless, be one-sided or wrong to suggest that Cyril's theology stood in opposition to that of the Council. His writings were, after all, cited with approval by the Council fathers, and all Chalcedonian churches have always insisted on the centrality of the Alexandrian bishop for their own Christological doctrine. A tension, however, can hardly be denied, and this tension went far beyond the terminological question of whether Cyril spoke of one or of two natures in the Incarnate Christ. It has as much to do with the formula of Chalcedon as it has with Cyril's teaching, not because the Council's teaching was wrong, but because any attempt to cast the truth about the person of Jesus into a rigid, dogmatic formula must inevitably remain ambivalent. Cyril as much as Luther may be said, in that precise sense, to stand on the boundary of what the Council of Chalcedon prescribed.

3 Luther and the Antiochene Tradition

At the same time, a case can be made against too far-reaching an identification of Luther's Christological position with that with Cyril and the Alexandrian tradition. Differences exist not merely in the sense that the two theologians obviously worked in vastly divergent theological and cultural contexts separated by more than one millennium, but also in more specific ways that can be instructive for understanding the specific character and the specific challenges of Luther's Christology.

To begin with, the Eucharistic opposition between Cyril and Nestorius was ultimately rather different from that between Luther and Zwingli. Both combatants in the fifth century accepted the real presence and, in fact, some form of transformation of the elements.[167] Even in his most polemical statements, therefore, Cyril did not complain that Nestorius denied the presence of Christ's body in the Eucharist; what he alleged was that his opponent could not explain why, together with the body of Christ, his divinity was present in the elements as well.[168] Luther and Zwingli, by contrast, both rejected transubstantiation; their disagreement, as we have seen, was solely about the presence of the body of Christ in the Lord's Supper. For Zwingli, the Eucharist was a memorial meal, and the real presence was therefore unimportant as well as implausible, whereas for Luther the mere possibility that Christ could somehow be present in his divinity but not in his body vitiated against the fundamental truth of the Incarnation.

The significance of Luther's insistence on the real presence, further, was less the need that Christians were nourished by "divinized flesh" in the Eucharist in order to receive incorruptibility (hence his opposition to transubstantiation), but the imperative that Christ's presence could only be real if it was the whole Christ, human as well as divine, who was present. Luther's unwillingness to compromise on this principle, however, was bound up with the whole of his Christology, as we have seen. In other words, it included the affirmation of Christ's solidarity with suffering humanity and, more broadly, the

---

167   Chadwick, "Christology and Eucharist in the Nestorian Controversy," 175, n. 1.

168   Cf. again the eleventh anathema, see n. 157 above.

insights developed under the title of the theology of the cross. To be sure, Christ's resurrected body for Luther was the body of glory, much as it was for Cyril; the reformer's argument for its ubiquity was evidently drawn from this fundamental consideration. Nevertheless, Luther could never permit this emphasis on the glory of the resurrected Christ to occlude the reality of his true human experience; even after Easter, the theology of the cross can never become a theology of glory.

We can at this point begin to see how, the similarities noted above between Cyril and Luther notwithstanding, the historical relationship between the two becomes more complex and potentially nearly reversed. While Luther followed the Alexandrian Father in his insistence on the need to prioritize the union of divine and human in the savior at almost all costs in order to account for human redemption, for his own reading of the gospel the emphasis on the full reality of Christ's human experience is of more importance than it was for Cyril.

Cyril – as Chadwick observed – "had little to say about the part played by Christ's soul in the Passion"[169] whereas Luther went out of his way to identify Christ's experience of agony and God-forsakenness with ours. A greater contrast can hardly be imagined.

---

169   Chadwick, "Christology and Eucharist in the Nestorian Controversy," 159.

Once it is conceded that Luther's and Cyril's positions are not fully the same, it becomes possible to perceive in Luther echoes of the heritage of Antiochene Christology, the tradition Cyril and his followers sought to suppress. Part of their opposition to the Alexandrian party was based on a rigid notion of divine impassibility and immutability; thus far, Luther's position is clearly aligned with Cyril's willingness to stress the paradoxical character of God's "suffering in the flesh" and the true humiliation (τα-πείνωσις) of the Logos in the Incarnation.

There is, however, another aspect. Nestorius, in responding to Cyril's charges, points out that Jesus does not say, "He who eats my divinity and drinks my divinity," but "he who eats my body and drinks my blood abides in me and I in him" (John 6, 56).[170] In other words, he was concerned that Cyril's Christology paid insufficient attention to Christ's humanity. It is not difficult to see how Luther would have sympathized with this observation.

Time and again, Nestorius emphasizes the importance of Christ's full and proper humanity. According to him, Hebrews 2, 11 ("He that sanctifies and they that are sanctified are one") shows the need of true solidarity between Christ's humanity and ours. The significance of the Eucharist, according to Cyril's opponent, lay in the fact that we are sanctified by a body that is taken from our common human-

---

170   Friedrich Loofs, *Nestoriana: Die Fragmente des Nestorius* (Halle: Niemeyer, 1905), 227, 24 – 228, 3.

ity. Since we are not divine ourselves, we depend on
the mediation of Christ to obtain salvation, but the
latter is possible only because there can be no doubt
that he was really and truly one of us.[171] Once again,
it is hard not to recognize an echo here of Luther's
insistence on the full compatibility of Christ's suffering with ours and his willingness to explore in detail
how this played out at the psychological level in particular.

This Antiochene tendency in Luther's Christology
plays out most explicitly in his language of divine-
human union. As Isaak August Dorner observed,
Luther throughout his career spoke of the person of
the savior not – as the Alexandrians would have done
– as the Logos uniting with himself human nature,
but of God and man united into one person: "The
union (*unio*) he regarded principally as a union of
natures, the result of which is the *unio personalis*."[172]
For all his Alexandrian, Cyrilline leanings, Luther
was ultimately keen to ensure that Christ's humanity
was as much part of the teaching of the Church as
his divinity. As much as his emphasis on the unity of
divine and human in the Incarnate mirrors the am-
bivalence of the great Alexandrian vis-à-vis Chalcedon, which was keenly felt by his followers in Egypt
and elsewhere, Luther's commitment to the full real-

---

171   Nestorius, *Liber Heraclides* 40.

172   Dorner, *Entwicklungsgeschichte der Lehre von der
       Person Christi*, 2nd part, 2nd ed. (Berlin: Schlawitz,
       1853), 539.

ity of Christ's human experience plays out in a way mirroring the tension between the teaching adopted by the Church in the wake of Chalcedon and the legacy of Antiochene theology. In both directions, as it were, he pushed against the limits imposed by the doctrinal formulae which, nonetheless, he accepted as a necessary part of the Church's tradition.

4 Conclusion

How can recounting the tensional history of Christology one thousand years before the Reformation help gauge the significance of Luther's Christology in its tensional relationship with the Chalcedonian tradition? Basil of Caesarea, the great Father of the fourth century, was asked in 376 to commit to the addition of a Christological formula to the Creed of Nicaea. His answer to this request by the fanatical Epiphanius of Salamis, is worth quoting here:

> But the teachings that have been added to that Creed about the Incarnation of the Lord we have neither examined into nor accepted, as being too deep for our comprehension, knowing that when we once alter the simplicity of the Creed we shall find no end of discussion, since the disputation will lead us ever on and on, and that we shall disturb the souls of the simpler folk by the introduction of what seems strange to them.[173]

173 Basil of Caesarea, *ep.* 258, 2; English translation as in Saint Basil, *The Letters*, trans. Roy J. Deferrari, vol.

In an astounding display of foresight, Basil was able
to anticipate the result of the attempt to adopt a
dogmatic formula defining the Church's Christological teaching. He was certainly right in terms of
the historical outcome; but what about the theological question underlying Basil's proposal? Would
the Church have fared better with no dogmatically
fixed Christology, as the great Father seems to have
thought? It is certainly the case that many other doctrinal topics, including absolutely central ones such
as the atonement, have never been decided in quite
the same rigidity.

Perhaps this would have been desirable, but the
history of the Church has shown over the centuries
that certain controversies cannot be contained even
if they lead to traumatic schism; the Reformation,
after all, is evidence for the same rule. More helpful,
then, may be a different observation. These conflicts
are so deep and fought over with so much passion
and without, seemingly, any ability to compromise
because fundamental issues are at stake on both
sides far beyond the particular doctrine at issue. In
other words, it is arguable that the conflictual history of Christology mirrors the unique importance
of the person of Jesus Christ for the entirety of the
Christian faith.

If this is true, however, it seems further plausible
that in each such instance something is lost as well

4, 41, Loeb Classical Library (London: Heinemann,
1926), with slight changes.

as gained. Each side emerges with a clearer sense of why they had to insist on their particular doctrinal point of view in order to preserve the full truth of Christianity, but this increase in clarity comes at the cost of losing sight of the perspective of the other. We thus arrive at a paradox: Christocentrism, the theological commitment to what Luther calls the principle of *Christ alone*, led to the formulation of the Christological dogma, but this very process also undermined its principal cause or justification as all resulting formulae fall short of expressing the full truth of the Christian confession to Jesus Christ.

Taking this insight seriously implies that the answer cannot be to dispense with doctrinal formulations but to recognize that they inevitably fall short of the fullness of the religious confession they are meant to articulate. In other words, recovering Chalcedonian Christology would involve both the willingness to adopt its language *and* an awareness of its insufficiency compared to the faith it was meant to express. Failing to do the former leads to the fiction of a "better" history of Christianity without doctrine; this has been a problem for much of liberal Christianity. Yet the opposite failure is serious as well, as it leads to a downward spiral of conceptually accomplished but spiritually vacuous and empty forms of theology, far removed from the reality of the lived faith on the basis of the confession to Christ alone.

Luther's Christology can be understood as an attempt to do justice to this paradoxical insight. He affirmed the validity of Chalcedon and clearly distanced himself from those, such as Caspar von Schwenckfeldt, who sought to replace it. Yet this affirmation for him was inseparable from the need to acknowledge and articulate the tension already built into the dogma between the richer Christocentric faith it seeks to express and its representation by the technical formula itself. It was precisely the failure of "scholasticism," in Luther's view, to have neglected the latter necessity, leading to an increasingly impoverished understanding of the faith, which, in its turn, had disastrous consequences for the life of the Church as a whole.

It is perhaps intriguing to take this argument one step further by observing how the narrowing down of the Church's full awareness of the role Jesus Christ has to play for her faith and life, which inevitably followed the dogmatic divisions of the fifth century, led to practical consequences that are not at all remote from those Luther addressed in the sixteenth century. One consequence of the theological path on which the Church was set by Cyril's high Christology was the growth in significance of the veneration of the Virgin Mary and of the saints in general.[174] Whatever the positive and important aspects of this development may have been, there clearly was a danger that the loss of Christ as the human brother was compensated for by another "figure in complete soli-

---

174   Chadwick, "Christology and Eucharist in the Nestorian Controversy," 162–64.

darity with us," as Henry Chadwick has called it.[175] The link with Luther's program of Reform is immediately evident: to restore the veneration of saints to its rightful place, it was imperative to have a Christology that allowed a place to the man Jesus as our human brother and, as such, "the one mediator who can reconcile God and humanity" (1 Tim 2, 5). No *solus Christus* without the fullest possible Christology.

---

175   Ibid.

5 CONCLUSION:
CHRIST ALONE AND THE
DOCTRINE OF CHRIST

Jesus of Nazareth was a human person, an historical individual who lived in the Roman province of
Palestine during the first century of the common era.
For Christianity, however, Jesus Christ was also, literally, everything: "whom all the world could not en-
wrap / lieth he in Mary's lap," as Luther expressed it
in one of his Christmas hymns.[176] Luther's attempts
to come to terms with the Christological heritage, as
we have seen, was entirely driven by his awareness
that both sides of this paradoxical reality have to be
expressed. His program of *solus Christus*, therefore,
brings to the fore tensions inherent in all Christologies – between Christ's humanity and his divinity;
between his personal unity and the duality of his
"natures"; between his individuality and his universal
significance. In this lecture, I have sought to suggest
that this tensional Christology, which Luther never
successfully synthesized into a coherent, systematic
doctrine, is the direct result of his uncompromising
Christocentric stance, and quite inevitably so given
the historical evidence for the divisive nature of past
attempts to agree on a single Christological formula.
I will now use this final section of my lecture to ar-

---

176   LW 53, 241.

gue for the same claim on the basis of a systematic reflection on this doctrine.

Christology has often been recognized as the most difficult, the most complex and possibly the most paradoxical of all the teachings the Christian Church has adopted. Yet when considered in the context of Luther's famous maxim of "Christ alone," we can perceive another layer of complexity that is not always in view when Christology is reflected on: it is a uniquely ambitious doctrine as it seeks to capture the fullness of this person and its absolute importance for the whole of Christian existence in abstract formulae. If Christology is difficult taken on its own, the notion that a doctrine of the person of Jesus Christ could fully underwrite the wealth of Christian beliefs and practices relating to this person considerably increases the sense that this doctrine seeks to achieve something impossible. In fact, the requirements of doctrinal purification and conceptual clarification, on the one hand, and the needs of a religious and spiritual life that is based on "Christ alone," seem to pull into altogether different directions. Small wonder, therefore, that Christology has both been hailed as the center of Christian doctrine *and* been singled out as the most untoward of the technicalities the early Fathers produced.

Samuel Taylor Coleridge famously called Christianity "a life":

> Christianity is not a theory or speculation, but a
> life; not a philosophy of life, but a life and living
> process.[177]

Theology, then, as the attempt to represent this life
in rational form, will never map easily onto its reality. In this sense, I have argued at the end of the
previous chapter that a tension between the technical refinement of dogma and the faith it is meant to
encapsulate is characteristic of doctrine in general.
The Church has consistently assumed that the principles of doctrine are the same as those of Christian
worship (*lex credendi, lex orandi*) but this statement
masks constant struggle and conflict over how to
keep those two in tandem.

Christology is the most important and the most
extreme test case for this general truth. Technical Christologies have, more than any other part of
Christian doctrine, led to distinctions and specula-
tive subtleties that seem far away from the lived practice of the Christian faith. Paradoxically, however,
this alienation of doctrinal Christology from the life
of the faith is also the direct result of its unique and
comprehensive significance for that faith. Luther, we
have seen, is dismissive of his "scholastic" and "philosophical" forebears; this reflects his insight that the
enormously sophisticated Christologies of the Ockhamists under whom he studied effectively stood in

---

177   Samuel Taylor Coleridge, *Aids to Reflection*, in
       Coleridge, *The Major Works*, ed. H. J. Jackson (Ox-
       ford: Oxford University Press, 1985), 670.

the way of a full and proper appreciation of Christ's unique importance for the Christian faith. Yet we can easily see how the same theologians would have defended themselves. They would have justified the intellectual effort put into even the smallest detail in their systematic accounts of this doctrine precisely by pointing to the centrality this doctrine has for the Christian faith. They would have claimed that in their own way they were as Christocentric as Luther claimed to be.

It is important to see that Luther does not simply disown the latter need. He does not opt for an anti-intellectual religion of the heart as opposed to the scientific theology of the scholastics. On the contrary, he unequivocally accepts the Christological doctrine of the early Church as the basis of his own Christocentric theology. He certainly is no forerunner of an undogmatic Christianity. He is, however, consciously and intentionally disowning the refined subtleties of his immediate theological predecessors in the interest of a Christology that is constantly kept close to the heart of the gospel as he understood it. One could here see a parallel to the intellectual tendency of the age of Renaissance and Humanism with its preference for practical matters over against purely intellectual speculation, but the similarities are ultimately limited. Luther's attempt is to recalibrate the balance between the doctrine of the Person of Jesus Christ and the comprehensive life it was meant to underwrite.

In this attempt, Luther could legitimately claim to hark back to the christologies of the Patristic age, especially up until the fifth century. While it is hard to offer firm evidence for his actual dependence on the Fathers, both his strong sense of the link between Christology and the totality of a Christocentric theology and his willingness to embrace, in this interest, a range of tensional tenets chime well with the doctrinal period prior to the cataclysmic divisions caused by the controversies from the fifth century onwards.

Yet Luther is not simply rehashing Patristic theologies. He has his own answer to the problem of the tension between the confession to Christ alone and Christological doctrine. This answer is evident in what throughout this lecture I have called the soteriological cast of his Christology or his soteriological approach to this doctrine. Neither of the two formulations, however, fully captures the systematic significance of Luther's decision. When looked at from the perspective of the inevitable tension between Christological doctrine and the life of the Christian faith, we can now see that this close connection between soteriology and Christology is more than the internal relationship between doctrines; it is an attempt to relate doctrine and faith, doctrine and the Christian life. Concepts such as faith, grace, and redemption are not, for Luther, primarily theological theories; they are expressions of the existential experience of the life of the believer. This is why they have to be particularly emphasized (*sola fide*; *sola gratia*); this is why justification by faith took on such a central role in Luther's thought. It is therefore unhelpful to present Luther as prioritizing some doctrines over others, however one may want to adjudicate his theological decisions. Rather, he saw the need to reestablish the equilibrium between faith and theology, or between the life of the believer and theology, which, he felt, had been unsettled in late scholasticism. His uncompromising focus on the gospel as the promise of salvation, in this perspective, is an insistence that experience and theology have to be held together.

This is not, arguably, the demotion of Christology to a secondary doctrine, but an attempt to reestablish its true significance by tying it together with the *solus Christus* as the center of Christian life in its entirety. By the same token, however, it is easy to see that Luther's teaching cannot be considered the ultimate solution to the problem. If Christology remains foundational as a doctrine, its internal coherence is a lasting concern, and Luther's rather cavalier attitude to it could not satisfy in the long run. It is therefore unsurprising that later generations of Lutheran theologians once again turned to the subtleties of this doctrine trying to resolve the tensions evident in their master's thought. Doctrinal conflict and divisions were recurrent throughout the later sixteenth and the seventeenth centuries until the emergence of Pietistic and Enlightenment theologians critiqued those earlier Lutherans as "scholastic" and affirmed, in their turn, theology's practical dimension as an antidote against empty speculation. This time, the pendulum decidedly swung away from doctrinal Christology, however. To his liberal admirers Luther appeared as an early advocate of the abolition of doctrine in favor of religious experience, and his protestations to the contrary were interpreted as mere nods to the doctrinal status quo of his time.

By contrast, Luther's own Christology, as we have seen, is driven by an awareness that the Christian faith needs doctrine and is guided by doctrine, but also depends on a close correlation between its theoretical articulation and the practical experience of the believer. For all its imperfections, it can therefore serve even today as the guardian on a middle way between the extremes of a barren dogmaticism and an undogmatic Christianity, both of which have seemed attractive to Christianity in past and present.

Quite how this middle path is pursued remains controversial in our own time. Luther's own emphatic interpretation held it to be incompatible with the ecclesiastical foundation established by Roman Catholicism, and Protestantism has followed him in this assessment. Others differed, and the consolidation and renovation of Catholicism following the Council of Trent is a stark and salutary reminder of the spiritual and intellectual strength of that opposition. Remembering Luther's contribution to the history of Christianity five hundred years later cannot and should not obscure the major differences that emerged at the time. While it is, admittedly, tempting to pretend that those conflicts were based on misunderstandings or on disagreement about doctrinal or practical minutiae that have long become obsolete, closer scrutiny reveals that the issues at stake, rather, were and remain of absolute centrality to the Christian Church. While we cannot hope that the present anniversary will provide ultimate solutions to them, it will serve its purpose if it leads both Catholics and Protestants to renewed reflection about the need to put Jesus Christ truly at the center of all aspects of their faith.

COMPLETE LIST OF THE
PÈRE MARQUETTE LECTURES

Quesnell, Quentin
The Authority for Authority
ISBN 0-87462-517-3 (1969, Lecture 1) 54 pp.

Macquarrie, John
Mystery and Truth
ISBN 0-87462-518- 1 (1970, Lecture 2) 48 pp.

Lonergan, Bernard, S.J.
Doctrinal Pluralism
ISBN 0-87462-503-3 (1971, Lecture 3) 82 pp.

Lindbeck, George A.
Infallibility
ISBN 0-87462-504-1 (1972, Lecture 4) 78 pp.

McCormick, Richard A., S.J.
Ambiguity in Moral Choice
ISBN 0-87462-505-X (1973 Lecture 5) 116 pp.

Dulles, Avery, S.J.
*Church Membership as a Catholic and
Ecumenical Problem*
ISBN 0-87462-506-8 (1974, Lecture 6) 118 pp.

Gustafson, James M.
The Contributions of Theology to
Medical Ethics
ISBN 0-87462-507-6 (1975, Lecture 7) 116 pp.

Tanenbaum, Marc H., Rabbi
Religious Values in an Age of Violence
ISBN 0-87462-508-4 (1976, Lecture 8) 64 pp.

Baum, Gregory
Truth Beyond Relativism:
Karl Mannheims Sociology of Knowledge
ISBN 0-87462-509-2 (1977, Lecture 9) 94 pp.

Maloney, George A., S.J.
A Theology of "Uncreated Energies"
ISBN 0-87462-516-5 (1978, Lecture 10) 142 pp.

Crowe, Frederick E., S.J.
Method in Theology:
An Organon for Our Time
ISBN 0-87462-519-X (1980, Lecture 11) 68 pp.

Hennesey, James, S.J.
Catholics in the Promised Land of the Saints
ISBN 0-87462-536-X (1981, Lecture 12) 50 pp.

Hellwig, Monika
Whose Experience Counts in
Theological Reflection?
ISBN 0-87462-537-8 (1982, Lecture 13) 112 pp.

Donahue, John R., S.J.
The Theology and Setting of Discipleship in the
Gospel of Mark
ISBN 0-87462-538-6 (1983, Lecture 14) 44 pp.

Hauerwas, Stanley
Should War Be Eliminated?
Philosophical and Theological Investigations
ISBN 0-87462-539-4 (1984, Lecture 15) 72 pp.

Orsy, Ladislas, S.J.
From Vision to Legislation:
From the Council to a Code of Laws
ISBN 0-87462-540-8 (1985, Lecture 16) 59 pp.

Brueggemann, Walter
Revelation and Violence:
A Study in Contextualization
ISBN 0-87462-541-6 (1986, Lecture 17) 70 pp.

Fogarty, Gerald
Nova Et Vetera: *The Theology of Tradition in American Catholicism*
ISBN 0-87462-542-4 (1987, Lecture 18) 79 pp.

Kasper, Walter
Christian Understanding of Freedom and History of Freedom in the Modern Era:
The Meeting and Confrontation between Christianity and the Modern Era in a Postmodern Situation
ISBN 0-87462-543-2 (1988, Lecture 19) 61 pp.

May, William E.
Moral Absolutes: *Catholic Tradition, Current Trends, and the Truth*
ISBN 0-87462-544-0 (1989, Lecture 20) 93 pp.

Collins, Adela Yarbro
Is Mark's Gospel a Life of Jesus?
ISBN 0-87462-545-9 (1990 Lecture 21) 77 pp.

Principe, Walter H., C.S.B.
Faith, History and Cultures:
Stability and Change in Church Teachings
ISBN 0-87462-546-7 (1991, Lecture 22) 63 pp.

Jaki, Stanley L., O.S.B.
Universe and Creed
ISBN 0-87462-547-5 (1992, Lecture 23) 86 pp.

O'Collins, Gerald, S.J.
The Resurrection of Jesus Christ:
Some Contemporary Issues
ISBN 0-87462-548-3 (1993, Lecture 24) 50 pp.

Weakland, Rembert G., O.S.B.
Seeking God in Contemporary Culture
ISBN 0-87462-549-1 (1994, Lecture 25) 45 pp.

Clifford, Richard J., S.J.
The Book of Proverbs and
Our Search for Wisdom
ISBN 0-87462-575-0 (1995, Lecture 26) 50 pp.

Fahey, Michael, S.J.
Orthodox and Catholic Sister Churches:
East Is West and West Is East
ISBN 0-87462-576-9 (1996, Lecture 27) 58 pp.

Griffith, Sidney H.
Faith Adoring the Mystery:
Reading the Bible with St. Ephraem the Syrian
ISBN 0-87462-577-7 (1997, Lecture 28) 56 pp.

Moltmann, Jurgen
Is There Life after Death?
ISBN 0-87462-578-5 (1998, Lecture 29) 60 pp.

Curran, Charles E.
Moral Theology at the end of the Century
ISBN 0-87462-579-3 (1999, Lecture 30) 60 pp.

Wainwright, Geoffrey
Is the Reformation over? Catholic and Protestants at
the Turn of the Millennia
ISBN 0-87462-580-7 (2000, Lecture 31) 86 pp.

Young, Robin Darling
In Procession Before the World: Martyrdom as
Public Liturgy in Early Christianity
ISBN 0-87462-581-5 (2001, Lecture 32) 80 pp.

Johnson, Luke Timothy
Septuagintal Midrash in the Speeches of Acts
ISBN 0-87462-582-3 (2002, Lecture 33) 72 pp.

Gy, Pierre-Marie
The Reception of Vatican II:
Liturgical Reforms in the Life of the Church
ISBN 0-87462-583-1 (2003, Lecture 34) 57 pp.

Cahill, Lisa Sowle
Bioethics and the Common Good
ISBN 0-87462-584-X (2004, Lecture 35) 88 pp.

Coffey, David
**"Did You Receive the Holy Spirit
When You Believed?"**
Some Basic Questions for Pneumatology.
ISBN 0-87462-585-8 (2005, Lecture 36) 125 pp.

Pesch, Otto Hermann
**The Ecumenical Potential of the
Second Vatican Council**
ISBN 0-87462-586-6 (2006, Lecture 37) 60 pp.

Rowland, Christopher
"Wheels within Wheels": *William Blake & Ezekiel's
Merkabah in Text & Image*
ISBN 13: 978-0-87462-587-5
ISBN 10: 0-87462-587-4 (2007, Lecture 38) 44 pp.

Komonchak, Joseph A.
Who Are the Church?
ISBN-13: 978-0-87462-588-2
ISBN-10: 0-87462-588-2 (2008, Lecture 39) 78 pp.

O'Regan, Cyril
Theology and the Spaces of Apocalyptic
ISBN-13: 978-0-87462-589-9
ISBN-10: 0-87462-589-0 (2009, Lecture 40) 160 pp.

Harvey, Susan Ashbrook
Song and Memory:
Biblical Women in Syriac Tradition
ISBN 978-0-87462-590-5 (2010, Lecture 41) 92 pp.

Levenson, Jon D.
Abraham between Torah and Gospel
ISBN 978-0-87462-592-9 (2011, Lecture 42) 79 pp.

Naughton, Michael
The Logic of Gift:
Rethinking Business as a Community of Persons
ISBN 978-0-87462-596-7 (2012, Lecture 43) 88 pp.

Marion, Jean-Luc
Givenness & Hermeneutics
Translated by Jean-Pierre Lafouge
ISBN 978-0-87462-598-1 (2013, Lecture 44) 81 pp.

Wilken, Robert Louis
The Christian Roots of Religious Freedom
ISBN 978-1-62600-500-6 (2014, Lecture 45) 48 pp.

J. Matthew Ashley
Take Lord and Receive All My Memory:
Toward an Anamnestic Mysticism
ISBN 978-1-62600-502-0 (2014, Lecture 46) 116 pp.

Larry W. Hurtado
***Why in the World Did Anyone Become a
Christian in the First Three Centuries?***
ISBN 978-1-62600-504-4 (2016, Lecture 47) 144 pp.

Johannes Zachhuber
***Luther's Christological Legacy
Christocentrism and the
Chalcedonian Tradition***
ISBN 978-1-62600-506-8 (2017, Lecture 48) 148 pp.

About the Père Marquette Lecture Series

The Annual Père Marquette Lecture Series began at Marquette University in the Spring of 1969. Ideal for classroom use, library additions, or private collections, the Père Marquette Lecture Series has received international acceptance by scholars, universities, and libraries. Hardbound in blue cloth with gold stamped covers. Uniform style and price ($15 each). Some reprints with soft covers. Regular reprinting keeps all volumes available. Ordering information (purchase orders, checks, and major credit cards accepted):

Marquette University Press
order Toll-Free (800) 247-6553
fax: (419) 281-6883
online: www.marquette.edu/mupress/

Editorial Address:
Dr. Andrew Tallon, Director
Marquette University Press
Box 3141
Milwaukee WI 53201-3141
phone: (414) 288-1564
email: andrew.tallon@marquette.edu
web: www.marquette.edu/mupress/